Flavor of the Month

Flavor of the Month

Why Smart People Fall for Fads

Joel Best

UNIVERSITY OF CALIFORNIA PRESS

Berkeley   Los Angeles   London

University of California Press, one of the most distinguished
university presses in the United States, enriches lives around
the world by advancing scholarship in the humanities, social
sciences, and natural sciences. Its activities are supported
by the UC Press Foundation and by philanthropic contributions from individuals and institutions. For more information, visit www.ucpress.edu.

University of California Press
Berkeley and Los Angeles, California

University of California Press, Ltd.
London, England

"Demotivator" on page 88 appears courtesy of Despair, Inc.
"Motivation" illustration by Kevin Sprouls.

Library of Congress Cataloging-in-Publication Data

Best, Joel.
    Flavor of the month : why smart people fall for fads / Joel
Best.
        p.   cm.
    Includes bibliographical references and index.
    ISBN 0-520-24626-8 (cloth : alk. paper).
    1. Social institutions.   2. Fads—Social aspects.
3. Diffusion of innovations.   I. Title.
HM826B.B47   2006
306—dc22   2005022128

Manufactured in the United States of America

15   14   13   12   11   10   09   08   07   06
10   9   8   7   6   5   4   3   2   1

This book is printed on Natures Book, which contains 50%
post-consumer waste and meets the minimum requirements
of ANSI/NISO Z39.48–1992 (R 1997) (*Permanence of Paper*). ♾

For Joan

Some enthusiasms are not
short-lived

Contents

Acknowledgments

I could not have—and would not have—written this book without the inspiration provided by various administrators at the three universities where I've spent nearly twenty-five years chairing academic departments. Department chairs attend many meetings at which the future is unveiled, priorities are articulated, and innovations are announced. Over the years, I have been assured that our university—if not all of higher education—was about to be transformed by affirmative action, the Pacific Rim, assessment, active learning, cooperative learning, distance learning, service learning, problem-based learning, responsibility-based management, zero-based budgeting, broadening the general education requirements, narrowing the general education requirements, capstone courses, writing across the curriculum, multicultural education, computer networking, the Internet, water (don't ask), critical thinking, quantitative reasoning, and I don't know what else. I have gone on retreats; participated in program reviews; served on task forces; puzzled over mission statements; written five-year plans, three-year plans, and niche reports; and listened to proclamations from provosts, assistant provosts, deans, associate deans, and wannabe deans. I have been assured with tight-lipped seriousness: "This is not a fad." Still, after all these amazing transformations, today's universities do not seem all that different than they were when I was a student. When I decided to write this book, I promised myself that I would not focus on fads in higher education because I suspected readers would consider the subject trivial, but I have to confess: that was where I discovered my topic. If I bear the scars of cynicism, I've earned them.

And I'm not alone. Sprinkled throughout this book are examples of anonymous "office folklore"—humorous works that circulate via photocopies and e-mail messages, and wind up displayed where we work. Folklorists have collected hundreds of examples of these works, many of which reveal at least skepticism, if not cynicism, about how our institutions operate. I'd like to thank those who created and improved these works, as well as those who only kept them in circulation until these bits of wisdom came to my attention; of course, the very nature of their contributions makes it impossible to credit these folks by name.

But there are others I can—and should—name. I want to thank the undergraduate and graduate students who helped me work through some of these ideas, particularly Theresa Appleby, Heather Smith Feldhaus, Karen McCready, and Tadashi Suzuki. The late Loy Bilderback, Sally Gergen, Rob Jensen, Milo Schield, and Richard Weiss all made helpful suggestions. Various drafts have also benefited greatly from comments by Benigno Aguirre, Joan Best, Katie Bogle, Gerald Bracey, Russell Dynes, Erich Goode, Carol Gregory, Chip Heath, Kath Lowney, E. L. Quarantelli, Eric Rise, David Schweingruber, and Richard Wilsnack. Once again, Victoria Becker helped transform my crude drawings into computer files. And, as always, Naomi Schneider, Sierra Filucci, Dore Brown, copyeditor Alice Falk, and the other people at the University of California Press improved the book and made the publishing process a good experience. These folks should be credited for trying to help me do better; the book's shortcomings are my own.

1

The Illusion of Diffusion

In the summer of 1958, our parents bought hula hoops, one for my younger brother and one for me. We weren't the first kids in our neighborhood to have them (I vaguely remember Dad having waited until the price dropped—hula hoops originally cost about $3, a lot of money in those days for some plastic tubing, a wooden plug, and two staples), but most of the kids I knew got one that summer.

I don't think we played all that much with our hula hoops. What I remember most were the photos that the newspapers and magazines ran that summer, pictures of other people having fun with the new toy. The first ones showed a young boy or girl spinning a hula hoop; but as the weeks passed, the photos displayed ever odder folks—a toddler with a hula hoop, a grandmother, a nun, someone spinning several hula hoops at the same time, groups of hula hoopers, and on and on. It seemed as though everyone had hula hoops.

And that was almost true. Sales were estimated at 25 million— one for every seven Americans, a hula hoop for every kid age 5 to 11 in 1958.[1] Then, almost as quickly as they appeared on the scene, hula hoops fell out of popularity. I remember ours, leaning forgotten against the garage wall, coated with dust.

FADS

Nearly half a century later, the hula hoop still is recalled as the prototypical fad—wildly popular, but short-lived. A graph* of its career might look something like this:

The Hula Hoop's Popularity— A Typical Fad

This graph shows that there was initially little interest in hula hoops; then their popularity rose quickly until it peaked, before rapidly dropping off again.

We could draw essentially the same graph for any fad, because these contours define the fad: a fad is a short-lived enthusiasm.[2] What makes something a fad is its rapid loss of popularity. This is an important point. People sometimes assume that fads share some quality, that they are by nature strange or silly or trivial. But

---

* The graphs in this chapter should be understood as approximations, much like the supply and demand curves drawn by economists. No one kept precise records of how the numbers of people who owned and used hula hoops—or wristwatches— shifted over time, so it is impossible to precisely reconstruct these changes. However, when sociologists are able to measure the popularity of novelties, their data generally display patterns similar to those shown in this chapter's graphs.

lots of things that seem strange at first catch on—tattoos and piercings are contemporary examples. A substantial and growing proportion of young, college-educated adults sport body decorations that would have seemed bizarre twenty years ago. What makes something a fad is not that it is peculiar but that it achieves short-lived popularity, only to fade away.

By and large, serious people don't feel they need to pay much attention to fads. We tend to dismiss fads as trivial, silly, inconsequential. When asked to name a fad, people tend to pick examples of young people playing—fad toys (hula hoops, Cabbage Patch Kids), dance fads (the twist, the Macarena), college students acting up (streaking, trying to set the record for the most people crammed into a phone booth), and the like.[3] We assume that fads aren't important because they seem so silly.

Yet we're also familiar with fads that aren't so frivolous, that people adopt with more serious intent. The most obvious examples are diet fads (new ways to eat and lose weight) and exercise fads (new ways to enhance health and fitness).[4] Often, they are promoted by people who seem to be experts—doctors, trainers, and the like. These promoters promise that this diet or exercise program will make a real difference, that we can shed those pounds, become fitter, and dramatically improve our lives. Of course, their solutions almost always turn out to be fads; our enthusiasm for these new sugar-busting, abs-crunching regimens tends to be short-lived. Many diet books and exercise machines wind up gathering dust—just like my old hula hoop.

Even serious professionals get caught up in what turn out to be short-term enthusiasms—that is, fads. Physicians go through periods when they favor particular diagnoses (disease fads) or therapies (treatment fads); managers adopt and then reject meth-

---

COULD THIS BE JUST A FAD?
Recent Article Titles in Professional Journals Reveal Doubts

From journals aimed at educators

"Career Academies: Cutting-Edge Reform or Passing Fad?" (2003)
"Online Learning: Fad or Fate?" (2001)

From medical journals

"Evidence-Based Medicine: A New Science or an Epidemiologic Fad?" (1999)
"Narrative-Based Medicine: A Passing Fad or a Giant Leap for General Practice?" (2003)

From management journals

"Is Empowerment Just a Fad?" (1997)
"Complexity and Management: Fad or Radical Challenge to Systems Thinking?" (2002)

Sources: Mittelsteadt and Reeves (2003), Rourke (2001); Bauchner (1999), Launer (2003); Malone (1997), Holbrook (2002).

---

ods for improving business practices (management fads); educators devise and then drop teaching techniques (educational fads); and so on. Within particular institutions, commentators acknowledge that fads occur; they even write articles with titles that ask whether some hot new development will prove to be just a fad (see box above).

What these commentators don't seem to notice is that the fads in their particular institution resemble the short-lived enthusiasms that occur elsewhere. In our society, most serious institutions—medicine, science, business, education, criminal justice, and so on—experience what we can call *institutional fads.*[5] These institutional fads, especially in business, education, and medicine, are this book's subject.

Institutional fads are not trivial; they have real consequences for our lives. Most of the time, our experiments with new diets or exercise programs have little lasting effect. But when we rely on the current child-rearing guru's advice for raising our kids, our families are affected by whatever passes for today's wisdom. When our children attend the local school, what they learn is shaped by that school's current policies regarding teaching practices and discipline. We depend on our doctors to use diagnoses and treatments that can help us, rather than following some worthless trend. Our work lives—even the continued existence of our jobs—can depend on which management scheme our employers adopt. Whenever our lives intersect with social institutions, we can be affected by whatever ideas—including short-lived fads—are circulating within those institutions.

FADS AND INNOVATIONS

Fads can fool us. The sociologist Emory Bogardus made what was probably the first serious study of fads. Each year between 1915 and 1924, he asked about a hundred people to name five current fads.[6] Not surprisingly, he found that most fads did not last long enough to make more than one list; only a few received mention in three successive years. One of these was "men's wrist watches."

Huh? How could Bogardus's respondents have called wrist-watches a fad? Looking back, this seems like a foolish mistake. But when they first appeared, wristwatches were considered silly novelties; after all, the pocket watch and chain, suspended from the waistcoat, were as fundamental an element of proper male attire as the necktie. Bogardus's respondents called the wristwatch a fad because they didn't expect it to find lasting favor. And experts agreed. In 1915, the *New York Times* covered the debate over wrist-watches at the National Retail Jewelers' Association convention, and quoted a delegate: "There's some excuse for a woman wearing her watch on her wrist . . . but a man . . . has plenty of pockets"; another declared, "The wrist watch will never be a common time-piece." A wristwatch manufacturer explained: "Some of those fellows [are] afraid the sales of wrist watches will hurt the sale of more expensive watches. That's all wrong. A man who has a wrist watch will also have a regular watch."[7]

Only now, knowing as we do that the wristwatch has become— along with the wedding ring—one of the most popular forms of male jewelry, can we imagine what must have happened.[8] Men must have discovered its advantages—that, in addition to being cheaper than the pocket watch, it was lighter, could be worn with-out a vest, and could be viewed without occupying a hand to re-move it from its pocket and open its case. Knowing what we now know, we aren't surprised that wristwatches endured; in fact, we can only marvel that some people once considered the wristwatch a fad.

We can imagine a graph that traces the growing popularity of the wristwatch:

The Wristwatch Spreads— Typical Diffusion

This is actually a familiar graph among social scientists: it is usually called the S-curve because of its shape.[9] Innovations—new products (like wristwatches) but also new ideas, new customs, all sorts of novelties—tend to spread slowly at first; then their popularity rapidly increases, before leveling off. This process is called *diffusion*. The S-curve is well-known because it fits the diffusion histories of so many successful innovations—if you trace the spread of telephones, or televisions, or VCRs, or whatever, the resulting graph usually forms an S-curve.

If we superimpose our two graphs—the one for fads, and the S-curve for diffusion—we see something interesting:

**Comparing the Dynamics
of Fads and Diffusion**

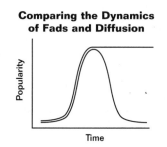

The process depicted on the left side of each graph is basically the same—in both cases, a few people adopt the novelty at first, followed by a rapid increase as lots of folks get involved, then a gradual tapering to a peak. Up to that point, there is essentially no difference between how fads (like hula hoops) and things that will prove to be lasting innovations (like wristwatches) spread. It is, of course, what happens next that makes the difference—fads soon lose popularity, while successful innovations remain popular.

Our wristwatch example reminds us of an important fact: initially, during the period shown on the left-hand side of our graphs, people can't be sure whether a novelty will endure or fade. Oh, sometimes they have a pretty good idea: it is hard to imagine that many people expected hula hoops to remain wildly popular, or thought that the telephone wouldn't last. But people's predictions are often wrong—and two sorts of mistakes are possible. The first error is what happened when Bogardus's respondents dismissed the wristwatch, or when 1950s adults insisted that rock and roll would soon disappear: that is, people predict that a novelty will be a fad, but it actually turns out to remain popular. The second mistake occurs when something is heralded as the newest important development, but it turns out to be a bust. There are lots of examples—remember CB radios? 8-track tapes? Betamax video recorders? In such cases, people experience what we'll call the *illusion of diffusion*—they expect an innovation to endure, only to be surprised when it loses popularity.

Most fads have enthusiasts who get caught up in this illusion. Think of the folks who thought Beanie Babies would be good long-term investments.[10] It is possible that Americans will permanently alter their eating habits in the ways envisioned by promoters of low-carb diets, but it seems at least as likely that low-carb will go the way of its various low-cal, low-sugar, and low-fat predecessors. While an innovation is spreading, we can't be sure what will happen next. This uncertainty about the future, about whether a novelty will prove to be a fad or a lasting innovation, is a central theme in this book. As we will see, the promoters of institutional fads often get caught up in the illusion of diffusion; they prefer to imagine that they're involved with important innovations rather than trivial fads.

HOW FADS DIFFER FROM FASHIONS

Just as we need to distinguish fads from the diffusion of success-ful innovations, we must make a distinction between fads and fashions. This is a confusing topic. The experts disagree: some argue that fad and fashion are two names for one phenomenon; others insist they are different, but can't agree on what the dif-ference is. Most often, they dismiss fads as "trifling or insignifi-cant," or "more trivial" than fashion.[11] Certainly some familiar fads (such as hula hoops and streaking) may seem trivial, but oth-ers—such as the institutional fads that are this book's focus—involve serious matters. But why call them fads instead of fash-ions? We need to understand how the two differ.

It may help to begin with the example that many people equate with the very word *fashion:* the world of high-status designers creating new dresses for wealthy women. Initially, this world involved haute couture firms located in Paris and a few other major cities that employed such famed designers as Chris-tian Dior and Coco Chanel, who created new outfits; these were displayed at seasonal—traditionally fall and spring—shows; the shows were covered—that is, both publicized and criticized—by the fashion press; some well-received designs actually became available as clothing that could be purchased from high-status vendors; and the styles that originated in this high-prestige venue gradually trickled down, adapted by a succession of in-creasingly less-prestigious manufacturers, to be sold by less-exclusive stores at ever cheaper prices, to women of ever lower status. The system has evolved; today, a designer may establish a reputation within the high-fashion world, then begin working with much less prestigious vendors (for example, Isaac Mizrahi designing lines for Target).[12] Still, many fashions display a familiar underlying process: designs with high-status origins spread to less-exclusive venues.

This trickle-down process was at the core of one of the first—and still one of the most influential—analyses of fashion, presented by the great German sociologist Georg Simmel in 1904.[13] Simmel's basic model envisioned society as a hierarchy or ladder, on which those at the top try to differentiate themselves from the people on the rung below them by adopting new symbols of their higher status (such as a new clothing fashion). But soon, those on the second rung begin to imitate their betters by themselves adopting those same symbols, thereby distinguishing themselves from the folks down on the third rung. This process is repeated as each successive rung of subordinates adopts the fashion of their superiors, only to have it copied by those below them in the hierarchy. And once subordinates adopt a fashion, it no longer serves to distinguish those above from those below, and the former must seek new symbols to set themselves apart from their inferiors. The result is a continual cycle in which those at the top of the status ladder adopt new fashions, only to be imitated by those on successively lower rungs.

Critics argue that Simmel's model does not fit contemporary fashions because modern society is too complex to be reduced to a single status ladder, and because our fashions often seem to begin among teenagers or others of modest status.[14] But ignore those criticisms for a moment, and imagine some particular fashion in clothing that obeys the trickle-down pattern—let's pick a year when the top designers declare that skirts will go up or go down or whatever. If we graph the trickle-down adoption of this fashion, we discover a familiar pattern. At the beginning, the new style is adopted by a few elite women, and then it spreads as it is adopted at increasing speed by larger numbers of women of ever lower status. By the time the new style has extended a few rungs down the ladder, those at the top are beginning to drop it; by the time the style achieves its greatest popularity among those of lower status, it is also losing favor in the middle ranks and will soon be dropped, so that we wind up with something much like our familiar fad graph. In other words, particular fashions display essentially the same dynamics as fads:

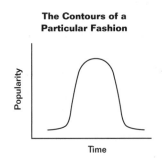

The Contours of a Particular Fashion

Popularity

Time

However, this cannot be the end of the matter. People do not drop a tired clothing style in favor of nakedness. Rather, during the next fashion season, they adopt some new style—even shorter skirts, or longer ones, or whatever the designers are now promoting. Thus, over time, we get a succession of styles, each rising in popularity and then falling as its successor rises: it is this repetitive sequence that distinguishes fashion from fads. Fads are *episodic*—one-shot enthusiasms. When hula hoops lose popularity, it is not necessarily true that something will come along to replace them.

Successive Fashions

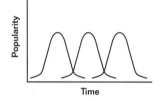

In contrast, fashion is *systematic*; it institutionalizes change, puts it on a schedule. As the critic Joseph Epstein says, "Fashion implies transience, but transience regularized."[15] The traditional high-fashion world illustrates this perfectly: its designers worked on a seasonal timetable to prepare new creations for the upcoming shows that would attract the fashion press and buyers. This world—in spite of all the hype about the designers' genius and originality and spontaneity—consisted of established businesses producing goods within a fixed routine. No one in the haute couture world imagined that the upcoming show's fashions would remain fashionable forever—the new designs were intended to be popular only for a season, before losing favor to the next scheduled inspiration.

Nor is high-fashion clothing unique. There are lots of what sociologists call "culture industries" that produce goods intended to achieve brief popularity, before being supplanted by something new.[16] Think about book publishers, or the people who produce movies or music. Nobody expects this week's number one best seller, top box-office draw, or chart-topping song to stay on top forever—or even for all that long. These are all fashion industries that depend on people's continually shifting tastes.

While fashion is systematic, it is not predictable. That is, while we know that six months from now, some new movie will out-gross the competition, we cannot be sure which film it will be.[17] This unpredictability is a characteristic of fashion: people hope that their dress designs, their books, or whatever they've created will become popular; they do everything they can to make this happen; but they cannot predict the outcome with complete confidence. Most books, songs, and dress designs will flop; a few will be hits, but nobody knows which ones will make it big. Inevitably, there are surprises. Consider the fates of two big-budget Holly-wood ocean epics. Movie industry observers confidently predicted that *Waterworld* (a Kevin Costner adventure movie) would outstrip the competition during the summer of 1995, while the buzz about 1997's *Titanic* was grim (naysayers warned that people wouldn't go to see a movie they knew would have an unhappy ending). But it was *Waterworld* that tanked, while *Titanic* sailed to box-office records. Or take the unexpected success of 2004's *Fahrenheit 9/11;* no one in the industry anticipated that the low-cost, polemical documentary would gross well over $100 million. People who work in fashion industries know that something will be fashionable—they just can't be sure what will hit and what will miss.[18]

Obviously, the line between fad and fashion cannot be drawn with precision. When we say that fads are episodic while fashions are systematic, we are describing a continuum, not an either-or dichotomy. Purely episodic fads are at one end of this continuum; they are one of a kind, each unlike any other fad. But we also can spot clusters of similar fads, such as college students acting up (panty raids, goldfish eating, telephone booth stuffing, streaking, rioting on Halloween or other festive occasions, etc.), toy fads (hula hoops, Rubik's cubes, Cabbage Patch Kids, etc.), or fad diets (low-sugar, low-fat, low-carb, etc.). Such *fad clusters* involve the same sorts of people (such as college kids), adopting roughly the same sorts of objects or activities (doing outrageous stuff), for essentially the same reasons (to have fun and attract attention). The similarities among the fads within these clusters are obvious; fads of these sorts aren't completely unrelated to one another.[19] Yet the similarities among a cluster of fads fall short of the elaborately organized systems we find in fashion industries. For example, as the winter holidays approach, the press often tries to pick this year's hot toy; they anticipate the appearance of a toy fad, even though most years don't have one.[20] In contrast, recall the highly structured world of high-fashion clothing—the same firms, with biannually scheduled shows, for the same audiences. The clusters of toy fads or campus fads aren't nearly so well organized. Some fads may be purely episodic, those in clusters less so, but fads remain more episodic than fashions.

Both fads and fashions are forms of fleeting or short-lived enthusiasms. That is, they achieve considerable popularity, but only briefly. In describing them as enthusiasms, I mean to suggest that people find them interesting and appealing. But I do not mean to imply that the people who adopt fads are irrational or out of control. As we will see, people often have quite rational reasons for participating in fads.

INSTITUTIONAL FADS

So far, we have contrasted fads with the diffusion of enduring innovations, and with the highly structured industries that produce fashions. All three phenomena—fads, diffusion, and fashion—involve the spread of new things, of novelties, and in each case there is uncertainty about the future. When some novelty is beginning to spread—when it's at the beginning of what will become either the typical fad/fashion graph or the standard diffusion S-curve—people can't be sure what's going to happen next: Will this novelty attract people's attention? If so, how long will interest in the novelty continue to grow; when will it taper off? And once interest peaks, will it remain high—a case of successful diffusion—or will it drop off, proving that the novelty was just a fad or fashion? No one can be sure of the answers to these questions in advance. Even within the most structured fashion industry, there is uncertainty about which items will rise to popularity, how popular they will become, and how long they will remain in vogue.

While such uncertainties may grip individuals who have a stake in promoting a particular fad or fashion, we might be excused for thinking it hardly matters. So long as we think of fads in terms of hula hoops, streaking, and other playful enthusiasms of the young, or of fashion in terms of which dress or movie proves most popular, we can dismiss fads and fashions as relatively unimportant. Since these inconsequential examples are what first come to mind when we think about fads and fashions, it is no wonder that we don't take either seriously.

However, institutional fads are another matter. They are endorsed by serious people—such as physicians, educators, and business leaders—who insist that the novelties they are promoting are important and will endure. Even if those predictions prove false, institutional fads can have serious consequences. Anyone who follows the news can spot examples of institutional fads. Consider three cases from the 1980s:

- Although a German physician first described multiple-personality disorder (MPD) in 1791, it remained an exceedingly rare diagnosis. In the half century before 1972, less than a dozen cases were reported in the United States; but during the 1980s, psychiatrists diagnosed thousands of cases. And whereas early cases almost always involved patients with only two personalities, the 1980s patients diagnosed with MPD often displayed dozens of "alters." Diagnoses have since fallen off. The 1980s epidemic of MPD was a *medical fad*.[21]

- During the 1970s and 1980s, business analysts worried that the Japanese economy was growing at a faster pace than that of the United States. Some suggested that Americans needed to appreciate and adopt Japanese business practices. In particular, hundreds of U.S. corporations announced that they would establish quality circles—groups that would allow workers and managers to discuss methods of improving quality. However, within a few years, quality circles had fallen out of favor; they had proven to be another *management fad*.[22]

- In 1989, there was great excitement when two University of Utah researchers declared that they had produced a cold fusion reaction in their laboratory. The implications seemed stupendous: once harnessed, cold fusion might provide a cheap, nonpolluting way to generate limitless energy. The scientists' announcement inspired considerable scientific activity around the world, while media commentators speculated about the tremendous impact this new energy source would have on society. But the researchers' results could not be replicated, and cold fusion is recalled as a short-lived *scientific fad*.[23]

The point is not that the 1980s was some sort of bizarre, fad-infested decade. I chose these examples because we now have a little distance from them. Today, when we look back on the excitement about the epidemic of multiple-personality disorder, quality circles' promise to transform American industry, or the wonders of cold fusion, these enthusiasms seem not just misplaced but strange and even silly. But we are less willing to label currently popular ideas as fads, even though an impartial observer might suspect that today's fascination with, say, Six Sigma management techniques, program assessment in higher education, or standardized testing to achieve educational accountability may seem a little odd ten or twenty years from now.

Psychiatrists, managers, and scientists are serious people, but in these three cases serious people bought into what, in retrospect, seem to have been strange ideas. Yet however peculiar institutional fads may seem in retrospect, their repercussions are no laughing matter. During the height of the enthusiasm for the multiple-personality disorder diagnosis, a patient who approached a physician and complained of fairly minor depression could wind up diagnosed with MPD, hospitalized for months, and heavily drugged. Corporations spent many millions trying to implement quality circles. In comparison, Utah's state legislature, which quickly allocated $5 million to maintain the state's lead in cold fusion research, got off cheaply. Institutional fads can gobble up time and money.

The illusion of diffusion plays a key role in institutional fads. Serious people almost always reject the notion that their new enthusiasm is just a passing fad or fashion. Rather, they shun both F-words. The hallmark of the institutional fad is the conviction that far from being a fad, this innovation represents progress—it is an improvement that will prove worthwhile and endure. Remember: the front half of the classic fad curve looks just like the beginning of the S-curve of diffusion. When an innovation is spreading, no one can be sure whether it will become an enduring instance of diffusion or will fade as a forgotten fad. But the faithful, those who believe in the novelty's promise, insist that this will be a lasting change. Doubters are dismissed as unimaginative cynics or recalcitrant stick-in-the-muds who are blind to the future's possibilities. While the innovation is spreading, it is easy to believe, to dismiss the skeptics.

Institutional fads seem strange or peculiar only in hindsight, after they have been discredited or at least have fallen out of favor. While they are spreading, institutional fads do not seem silly or crazy. Rather, they are promoted as sane, rational improvements. Their proponents often are respected figures in their professions, and their claims receive serious, deferential attention in the media. It is only later, after the enthusiasm has died down, that people point to the idea's flaws and recognize that this was, after all, just another fad.

Some observers, particularly in the business world, dislike the word *fad*. They prefer to speak of *management fashion*, a term that seems more dignified, classier (remember the glossy, high-status Parisian fashion world), less frivolous. But in our terms, institutional fads are fads, not fashions, because they are basically episodic and not systematic. The newest management approach is presented not as this season's management style but as a solid, rational, lasting solution. To be sure, there is a cluster for management fads, just as there is for college fads, but they are best understood as episodic rather than as the products of an ongoing fashion system.

Unlike hula hoops, institutional fads have serious consequences. These fads aren't free. Just as "fashion victims" waste their money on unattractive clothing styles, there are *fad victims* who suffer the costs of institutional fads. We've already noted that institutional fads consume resources: when an organization invests its people's time and money in adopting some new management scheme, alternative uses for those resources fall by the wayside. These are the prices that organizations pay for fads. Moreover, when the people who work in institutions watch fads get introduced with great fanfare, only to see them soon fall out of favor, alienation and cynicism can result. Soon, innovations are being dismissed as "the flavor of the month." Consider one of those pieces of humorous bureaucratic folklore that people post in their offices, reproduced in the box on page 20. "The Six Stages of a Project" has circulated, in slightly different forms, for decades; the author of the original version is unknown. It is, of course, a joke—but a joke with a serious message. It presents a cyclical—and cynical—view of organizational innovation, one that sees enthusiasm as not just temporary but illusionary.[24] People who post it in their offices proclaim themselves as jaded, as having seen it all before, and therefore as reluctant to buy into the next new thing. Thus, in a curious way, experience with institutional fads, which proclaim the possibility of change, may make

OFFICE FOLKLORE ON INSTITUTIONAL FADS

The Six Stages of a Project

1. Wild Enthusiasm
2. Disillusionment
3. Total Confusion
4. Search for the Guilty
5. Persecution of the Innocent
6. Praise and Honor for the Nonparticipants

people disillusioned—more suspicious of and resistant to calls for change. These are the prices paid by the people who work in institutions affected by fads: everyone—from the organization's top leaders to its lowest-ranking employee—risks becoming a fad victim.

But institutional fads are not restricted to the workplace. They intrude on our personal lives. Individuals find themselves trying to keep up with shifts in expert opinion. How should infants and children be raised? What are the health effects of different foods or beverages? What is the best way to lose weight? What should we do to find and maintain loving relationships? How should we invest for the future? Experts offer plenty of answers for these questions, but they often contradict one another, and opinions seem to shift over time—even from week to week. Trying to keep up with this fluctuating advice is a price we all pay for institutional fads—we all find ourselves, at least occasionally, becoming fad victims.

In short, contemporary institutions often seem to be characterized by a churning process in which some novelty, only yesterday heralded with great fanfare as the enduring solution to our problems, has fallen out of favor today, and is on its way to being forgotten by tomorrow. How can we explain this constant turnover?[25] What are its causes, and what are its consequences?

PLAN OF THE BOOK

This book seeks to answer these questions. Chapter 2 begins by considering how our culture—the basic assumptions we make about how the world works—provides a foundation upon which institutional fads can be assembled. Our beliefs in change, progress, and rationality make us willing to listen to proposals to make things better. We believe that change is often for the good, and therefore we welcome all sorts of novelties, including those that turn out to be institutional fads.

The next three chapters trace three stages in the trajectory or life cycle of institutional fads—emerging, surging, and purging. Chapter 3 examines *emerging*—institutional fads' origins, how they are created and launched. Often, a particular guru is credited with starting a fad; but for every successful promoter, there are many wannabe gurus whose ideas never take hold. Why do some ideas attract attention, while others fail to catch on? The answers lie in the ways contemporary institutions are organized, and in the social networks and media that foster the spread of novelties.

Chapter 4 addresses the next stage—*surging*—when people adopt a novel idea and cause it to spread. The motives of these individuals vary: some are true believers, convinced by and committed to the new scheme; others may be far less enthusiastic, even skeptical, yet still find themselves joining the cause. Here, we will focus on social psychology, on the enthusiasm that characterizes fads, the various reasons people buy into novelties, and the things they expect to gain from getting on the bandwagon.

Chapter 5 explores the key, final stage in the process—*purging*—when the fad peaks and declines. This is when the illusion of diffusion stands revealed, when the novelty's bright prospects dim. What causes a fad to lose adherents? While the answer might seem obvious—the novelty didn't work as promised—that turns out to be too simple a response to a rather complicated question. Fads fade not so much because they fail as because they age, lose the glamour associated with novelties, and become boring.

In chapter 6, our focus will expand to the larger topic of fad dynamics. People sometimes claim that social change resembles a swinging pendulum, oscillating between one extreme and another. Are there conditions that cause this pattern to emerge within institutions? Are there other conditions that cause different patterns to appear? In particular, when do institutions have difficulty shedding novel programs that don't work all that well?

Finally, chapter 7 tries to assess the impact of institutional fads. Defenders argue that these fads play a valuable, even necessary role in social progress, while their critics depict them as without value. This chapter also offers some suggestions for fad-proofing, for finding a middle ground between rejecting all innovation and being vulnerable to every passing enthusiasm.

2

Why We Embrace Novelties

Conditions That Foster
Institutional Fads

———

Next September, about 4 million youngsters will enter first grade in the United States. Their parents—and the rest of us—hope and expect that during the coming year, those first-graders will learn to read. In our society, the ability to read has become a fundamental, essential skill. A century ago, when people spoke of being illiterate, they meant someone who could not read or write more than his or her own name. Today, we worry about *functional illiteracy*—that is, the inability to read well enough to decipher a job application, an instruction manual, a tax form, or other basic documents. We have raised the bar: someone who reads well enough to have been thought literate a century ago may well be considered functionally illiterate today.

Fast-forward about four and a half years, when our beginning first-graders will be approaching the end of fifth grade. When they take tests to measure their reading skills, we can foresee the outcome. Some of them will be very good readers, and their parents will be proud to learn that their children are reading "above grade level." Other kids will be reading "at grade level"—doing as well as educators judge that children completing fifth grade should be able to read. But, predictably, there will be some whose performance lags "below grade level."

Because learning to read is so basic, so important, these less adept readers will likely become the focus of newspaper editorials and calls to do something about our "failing schools." In recent years, politicians from both parties have been insisting that America's schools must "leave no child behind." But our lagging fifth-graders will be evidence that some children still are being left behind, a situation that will probably inspire a lot of finger-pointing at the usual suspects: television; parents who let their children watch television and don't encourage them to read; teachers who aren't doing enough, perhaps because they aren't paid enough or aren't properly trained or don't care enough; principals who don't do enough to ensure that the teachers in their schools do enough; school systems that don't foster learning; legislators who don't support good schools; publishers who fail to produce books that will grab children's interest; and so on.

Sound familiar? Critics have been attacking schools' shortcomings throughout much of American history. We want our schools to do all sorts of things—to teach reading, but also to make children healthier, to encourage them to become good citizens, and so on. Thus, there is a long history of calls for reforms to improve education, demanding better ways of teaching not just reading but physical education, sex education, vocational education, and the like.[1] The recent enthusiasm for using standardized tests to foster academic achievement is simply one more installment in the long story of school reform.

People take these campaigns to improve education seriously because they invoke fundamental ideas in our culture, ideas about the possibility and desirability of change. Our ideas about change provide a cultural foundation for institutional fads. For example, our dissatisfaction with the flaws in today's schools, our conviction that schools could do a better job, and our desire to improve education for future children make us receptive to proposals for educational reform. This is why I can confidently predict that five years from now, those unacceptable, below-grade-level reading scores will be used to justify calls for new solutions to our schools' problems (although I can't know which proposals will become most popular). And we can also be fairly certain that those reforms will, in turn, fall short and the enthusiasm for them will prove to be short-lived, that they will become educational fads. In other words, fads in education and other institutions do not come out of the blue. Rather, institutional fads are founded upon some of our most basic, taken-for-granted beliefs about how the world should work and how we can make it better. This chapter begins by examining those ideas, then turns to some social conditions that also foster fads' spread.

Although this chapter focuses on American culture and society, I do not mean to suggest that the United States is uniquely susceptible to institutional fads. Rather, we should expect institutional fads to occur in other countries to the degree that their cultures and societies resemble ours.[2] That is, institutional fads will be common in all societies that welcome change, but rare where change is resisted.

IDEAS ABOUT CHANGE

We live, the cliché goes, in fast-changing times.[3] That's true. What we tend to forget is that it has been true throughout U.S. history. Americans have always had to deal with change, and they often worried about it: those newfangled railroads, critics warned, propelled people at unnatural speeds that threatened their health; and there were those who insisted that women were happier without the vote. Probably every change—every new invention, new law, new social arrangement—inspires opposition, or at least anxiety. There are always critics, doubters, and worriers who warn that a given change will make things worse.

The most extreme versions of our doubts about change involve doomsday scenarios—ecological devastation, economic collapse, war, plague, and famine—but we also hear warnings about plenty of less apocalyptic threats, such as the declining middle class, growing immorality, increasing political apathy, and so on. Even the most popular changes present challenges. New inventions—automobiles one hundred years ago, cell phones today—alter personal relationships, business transactions, and who knows what else. Faster transportation and communication make it easier to spread new ideas and new products, but also new diseases and new problems. We have the sense that a constantly changing world can and will shift in unexpected, unpredictable ways, and that we need to be nimble enough to adjust.

Our awareness that the world is continually changing makes us susceptible to claims that what we've been doing is no longer good enough, that we need to start doing something different. We may imagine that sometime back in the good old days, schools successfully taught first-graders to read, but we also suspect that those traditional teaching methods may no longer work because today's kids pose new challenges to educators and require new methods of instruction. And, remember, we worry that the stakes are now higher, that today's poor readers risk being condemned to marginal lives of poverty, so it is vital that we find better ways to teach reading.

Our concerns about change, then, help justify institutional fads.[4] Not just new teaching methods but new management strategies, as well as new approaches to such intimate parts of our lives as courtship, parenting, and eating, can be justified as responses to a changing world. We can't count on the traditional ways of doing things, because we fear that however well they may have worked in the past, the old ways don't fit our new, fast-changing world. Still, even as we worry that things may be changing for the worse, we also recognize that many changes in the past actually turned out for the better.

The Experience of Progress

Americans usually describe their history in terms of progress.[5] Most would agree that over time, things in the United States have gotten better. Our nation's story is one of geographic expansion, of pioneers settling the wilderness and eventually building great cities. It is a story of advancing technology, of the invention of the cotton gin and the telegraph, the telephone and the airplane. It tells of civic progress, greater civil liberties, public schools for all children, and the rise of Social Security. It is about the emergence of a great nation, one that had to fight first a revolution to win its freedom and then a civil war to end slavery, and that went on to become one of the world's superpowers. It is, in short, easy to present American history as a tale of progress.

Talk like this makes some people—particularly some intellec-
tuals—nervous and uncomfortable. They warn that our society
has been on a binge, a joyride, that we aren't paying attention,
that things aren't as good as they seem and are about to get a lot
worse. Many liberal critics believe they have a responsibility to
serve as society's conscience, to point out the ways in which social
arrangements are inequitable and unjust, and to speak up for the
vulnerable.[6] Talking about progress, they fear, invites complacency; it ignores those who were harmed in the past, and encourages people to ignore the plight of the less fortunate. For such
liberal critics, American history is a story of injustice—of Native
Americans being driven off their ancestral lands, of Africans
dragged to the New World in chains, and of poor people ex-
ploited by the rich.

Similarly, there are conservative critics who warn that appear-
ances of progress are superficial and mask underlying decline,
corruption, and decay.[7] They worry that children no longer
respect their parents, schools no longer teach the basics, and reli-
gion and law no longer command respect. They call for a return
to higher standards, to the enduring values that guided our an-
cestors. The alternative is continued decline and eventual collapse; for these conservative critics, the fall of the Roman Empire
illustrates the risks of complacency.

Both liberal and conservative critics, then, question claims
about progress; in some cases, they insist that things are actually
getting worse. Unfortunately, the critics' pessimism runs counter
to most Americans' lived experiences. Consider the United States
just one hundred years ago, when newborn infants had a life
expectancy of forty-some years, the great majority of Americans
left school by the time they finished eighth grade, relatively few

had electric power or indoor plumbing in their homes, telephones and automobiles were uncommon, women could vote in only a few states, and few African American males living in the former Confederacy could exercise the right to vote theoretically possessed by all men who were 21 and over.

A lot has changed in the past hundred years, and an awful lot of things changed for the better.[8] Life expectancies increased by almost thirty years for newborn males, and even more for females (with life expectancy rising more for nonwhites than for whites). The great majority of American teens now graduate from high school, and roughly a third of young adult Americans earn degrees from four-year colleges. The right to vote is generally available to all citizens ages 18 and over. The standard of living is vastly higher. Longer life expectancy, better education, an expanded right to vote, and a higher standard of living are bedrock social indicators. Who seriously wants to argue that these improvements don't represent progress?

Of course, we can't remember back a hundred years, but the experience of progress does not require such a long historical memory. Today's teenagers are bored by their parents' recollections of a world without cell phones, PCs, CDs, DVDs, PDAs, MP3s, and so on. We all have firsthand experience with progress, at least in this sense of witnessing the spread of new gadgets. We all accept the idea that things change, and most of us think that a lot of those changes have been for the good.

Obviously, this is not to say that we do—or should—believe that things get better every day in every way. Progress itself often creates new problems; we may be better off with cars than we were without them, but having cars means increased air pollution, traffic jams, motor vehicle accidents, and other challenges that

EDUCATORS ANTICIPATE PROGRESS
FROM NEW TECHNOLOGIES

"The motion picture is destined to revolutionize our educational system and . . . in a few years it will supplant largely, if not entirely, the use of textbooks." (1922)

"The possibilities of the radio in the educational field make every far-seeing, wide-awake school administrator from time to time indulge in fascinating dreams as to what may be done with this newest giant among modern inventions." (1930)

"We must be sure that education is in a position to obtain the full benefits that TV is capable of giving. . . . [U]ltimately all large school systems will have video stations. . . . Such an eventuality would permit the launching of really effective programs of instruction, in-service training, public relations work, promotion of scholastic athletics, and many other desirable projects." (1948)

"The potential is there to make the classroom a more imaginative and challenging learning environment with computers." (1980)

Sources: Tyack and Cuban (1995: 111); Emery (1930: 59); P. Lewis (1948: 158); Martellaro (1980: 104).

can be addressed only through further changes that, in turn, should lead to more progress.[9] Nearly everyone looks at the world and sees room for improvement. Even the critics most skeptical of progress demand change: liberals want society to become more just, while conservatives call for a revival of moral standards. But that's the point. Because we believe in progress, we believe that things can be improved, and that belief makes us willing to listen to people who claim they can show us how to make things better. We believe, for instance, that our schools can transform education by adopting new technologies (see box above).

This optimism that runs through our culture provides the basic foundation upon which institutional fads can be built. We think our institutions can get better, we think they should get better, and therefore we are willing to listen to proposals for improving things. In fact, we tend to become suspicious of stability, simply because stability is the absence of progress: if things aren't getting better, then there must be something wrong.[10] No wonder institutional fads catch on—in our culture, people are eager to experience something new and better.

Perfectibility as a Standard

What's more, we tend to judge our progress against a tough standard—perfection. This is, after all, what it means when we declare that our schools should leave no child behind, that every fifth-grader should be a good reader. Social perfectibility has long been a central theme in American culture. The Puritans envisioned creating a community of saints. The founders sought to devise not just a new but an ideal form of government. The nineteenth century produced great campaigns for social reform, as well as attempts to establish separate ideal communities, such as the Mormon Zion and many smaller utopian experiments. The belief that principled, committed people could create an ideal society continued to shape twentieth-century politics— the New Deal, the Fair Deal, the Great Society, the civil rights movement, and all of the other movements for the rights of women, children, gays and lesbians, the disabled, the elderly, and on and on. In recent decades, Americans declared war on poverty, cancer, and drugs. We are not naive: we don't necessarily expect to achieve perfection, but we are willing to declare it as our goal, to strive for it, and to measure our progress against it.

In fact, we have experience with solutions that, if not perfect, are at least close to it. When I was a boy, my parents lived in dread that my brother or I might contract polio—a mysterious disease that crippled and killed children, seemingly at random. One hundred years ago, the list of the ten diseases that caused the greatest number of deaths included measles—measles! A hundred years before that, the world was suffering from a centuries-long plague of smallpox. But polio, measles, and smallpox have been brought under something approaching complete control. Such dramatic successes teach an important lesson: it is possible to make some problems virtually disappear. Why shouldn't we aspire to perfection?

The problem, of course, is that perfection is an awfully high standard. It is all very well to announce that our schools will leave no child behind, but we can be pretty sure that there will be fifth-graders who aren't reading especially well five years from now, and ten years from now, and on into the future. We may aspire to perfection, but probably, most of the time, we aren't going to achieve it.

This means that our schools will always be seen as falling short, so long as they fail to teach some students, just as our hospitals will always fail to cure some patients, our prisons will fail to reform some inmates, and so on. In a sense, these are intractable problems.[11] That is, we recognize a persistent gap between what we want our institutions to accomplish and what they are actually able to do. This gap between perfection and what exists serves to justify calls for change—and institutional fads.

In spite of our history of progress, polls show that Americans' confidence in their institutions has fallen in recent decades. The gulf between the reality that is and the perfection that we desire, coupled with constant critiques from critics both inside and outside institutions, creates tension, strain, anxiety—pressure within those institutions to do more, and to do it better. This anxiety is at the root of institutional fads—"We aren't doing as well as we should be! We need to change, to get better!" A concern with falling short is found in education, medicine, and the other institutions that are susceptible to institutional fads.[12]

Perfectibility, then, is a two-edged sword. It serves to inspire us, when we declare war on poverty or cancer, when we promise to leave no child behind, or when we commit ourselves to finding a cure for AIDS. Yet at the same time, we can turn perfectibility into a club with which we can beat ourselves. Even if we have had great triumphs—such as almost wiping out polio—we are a long way from conquering disease. Even if we could cut the proportion of fifth-grade students reading below grade level in half, there will still be kids who aren't reading well enough, who are being left behind. It is this gap—this inevitable gap—between the perfectibility to which we aspire and what we are able to achieve that guarantees our receptiveness to proposals for change, and therefore to institutional fads.

Thinking Big: The Appeal of Revolution

Because Americans have confidence in the possibility of progress, and because we have perfection as a goal, our society is open to proponents of change. Our history celebrates the inventors, entrepreneurs, visionaries, and reformers who've promoted change: the founders who broke with Britain, crafted their own method of government, and established a new nation; Edison and the Wright brothers; Martin Luther King Jr.—the list goes on and on. Their stories remind us that while change does not necessarily come easily ("They laughed at the Wright brothers"), nonetheless it can transform our world.

At least change sometimes has that power. Our history is littered with failures, as well as successes—with inventions that never took hold; short-lived utopian communities; cults that never caught on; long-forgotten dietary, exercise, and health regimens; and unsuccessful social movements. Their stories now strike us as silly or sad, pathetic or just weird.[13] Campaigns to change things don't always work. They may have laughed at the Wright brothers, but they also mocked a lot of folks who are now forgotten.

When visionaries announce that they have discovered a new and better way, and try to interest and enlist others in their cause, the eventual outcomes can't be foreseen. Every person advocating change can find inspiration in the lessons of history: you have to keep trying ("It took Edison thousands of failed experiments before he devised a working lightbulb"); you may encounter opposition ("Dr. King faced violent mobs"); and so on. You have to believe in yourself, you have to be brave, you have to persevere.

These are powerful lessons, because they offer inspiration for struggling innovators. They give people who want to promote change plenty of models—admired figures, visionaries who once dared to think new thoughts and who became cultural heroes. Would-be innovators can imagine themselves following that same glorious path. There is—at least there can be—great honor in being an innovator; of course, you also can flop and wind up forgotten.

Our aspiration to perfectibility inspires people to think big, to promote even the most far-reaching changes. For Americans, the word *revolution* conjures not visions of bomb-throwing anarchists so much as the American Revolution, the Industrial Revolution, or the sexual revolution—all widely viewed as part of our history of progress. Advertisers would not promise that their cleanser offers "revolutionary new cleaning power" if they thought that the R-word would frighten consumers.[14]

Because of the positive value given to revolution, would-be reformers can dare to think big. They can challenge the taken-for-granted, argue that the familiar way we do things is simply wrong, and advocate something completely different. They can promise dramatic changes. To be sure, their proposals often will be rejected, and they will find themselves spurned as nuts, cranks, or quacks. But sometimes—sometimes—a radical new idea will take hold. History tells us so.

Our society makes a place for innovators: it gives them a chance; it is more open to advocacy of change than are many other societies. This, too, is part of the culture that supports institutional fads. There is an awareness that advocating change—even revolutionary transformations—sometimes proves to be right. And history's lessons are not just for the visionaries but for their audiences, too. It may have been fun to be part of the crowd jeering the first horseless carriage, but the smart money got out of the buggy whip business. We need to consider what the activists and agitators have to say—they might be on to something.

We celebrate dramatic breakthroughs. One of the greatest shifts in the history of scientific thinking occurred when astronomers abandoned the notion that the Sun, planets, and stars revolved about Earth in favor of the Copernican interpretation (in which Earth and the other planets are understood to revolve around the Sun). This new thesis was resisted by religious authorities who saw it as challenging doctrines that Earth and especially humans were the central focus of God's attention. When Thomas Kuhn, the historian of science, called this scientific revolution a *paradigm shift*, he was talking about a monumental change in the way people thought.[15] Kuhn's term caught on—so much so that it has become trivialized, and has lost its power (see box on p. 37). Speaking of shifting paradigms has become—like revolutionary changes, dramatic breakthroughs, or epochal shifts—just another clichéd way to exaggerate the importance of new developments.[16]

Such talk of dramatic breakthroughs taps into our belief in progress and perfectibility. If we're going to achieve a new and better world, we will need to do things very differently. The old ways have carried us as far as they can (and there's still that gap between our aspirations and our achievement); now we need to try something completely different. Often, there are overtones of urgency—we must act now, we can't afford to wait, because things will soon get worse and we'll fall further behind. This is what many institutional fads offer—the promise of a sudden, wonder-working, paradigm-shifting, revolutionary, quantum-leap breakthrough, a transformation that can make everything vastly better: the secret to students becoming better readers, businesses becoming more profitable, the sick being made well, or whatever.

JOURNALISTS ANNOUNCE RECENT PARADIGM SHIFTS IN VARIOUS INSTITUTIONS

In medicine:

"aggressively promoting orthodontic treatment [represents a] paradigm shift [for] orthodontics" (2004)

"a significant paradigm shift in physician appointment-scheduling philosophy" (2004)

In sports:

"the pat explanation for soccer's paradigm shift is that international-level success, circa 2004, is based more on conditioning and less on skill" (2004)

"the paradigm shift in premium [golf] balls from wound to solid-core construction" (2004)

In business:

"a paradigm shift in airline food service" (2003)

"a paradigm shift – from a seller's market to a buyer's market [in real estate]" (2002)

In consumer products:

"[playing music on] mobile phones [is] creating a . . . paradigm shift" (2004)

"[TiVo is] more than just a paradigm shift" (2004)

In – who knows?

"a paradigm shift from the traditional A/R management approaches of PFS to revenue cycle management accountability across the organization" (2004)

Sources: Hans (2004: 143), Jag Gill (2004); Wahl (2004: 68), *Golf* (2004: 104); Sharkey (2003: C7), Rozhon (2002: sec. 1, 43); R. Simon and Babinet (2004: 9), Taub (2004: G1); Healthcare Financial Management (2004: 53).

Faith in Rationality

We attribute progress, from garden-variety improvements to revolutionary transformations, to rationality. That is, we believe that our problems can be solved through reasoning rather than faith and that we can, through the application of rational principles, identify both the causes of those problems and better solutions to them. Our modern way of life—characterized by personal computers and MRIs—is a monument to the expansion and application of rational knowledge. Universities play a key role in this process; not only do they provide a setting for research that can generate new knowledge, but they also spread this information as they train the new professionals who will enter medicine, science, business, education, and other institutions.

Not all societies and institutions rely so heavily on rationality as a justification for doing things. Anthropologists describe groups that turn to witch doctors for cures and seers for prophecies. Similarly, religious leaders sometimes justify resisting changes by referring to unchanging, divinely inspired doctrines. But Americans tend to be impatient with those who can't accept the value of rationality and progress. When we read world history, we find many examples of institutions that—in our eyes— seem to have adopted wrongheaded policies: they prized tradition over progress, tried to govern through ritual and fixed doctrines rather than adapting to changing circumstances, and actively resisted and even sought to suppress novel ideas. Given our culture's deep belief in progress, such recalcitrance strikes us as foolish, doomed efforts to hold back the inevitable tide of the future. We disparage superstitions that block the benefits of science, generals who plan to fight the previous war instead of keeping up with advances in technology and tactics, and cultures that refuse to let women learn and fulfill their potential as contributors to society. Our sympathies are with Galileo, not his inquisitors. We have little patience for hidebound, stick-in-the-mud traditionalists who dismiss rationality and reject progress.[17]

Rationality also offers a basis for assessing change. We usually evaluate progress in terms of such yardsticks as productivity, efficiency, profitability, or effectiveness. Thus, efforts to promote "greener" business practices are justified not because they are ethically right but because they are said to produce measurable, practical benefits.[18] Most modern institutions, including business, science, medicine, and education, declare their ideological commitment to rational evaluation and planning.[19] In this view, only those changes that can produce measurable improvements should survive.

In short, our culture lets many new ideas get a hearing, rather than dismissing them out of hand. We grant the possibility that somebody could figure out a better way of doing things. We believe that change is inevitable, that progress is possible, that we should aspire to perfectibility, that revolutionary breakthroughs can occur, and that these improvements can be guided by rationality. Ours is an optimistic creed, one that looks to the future.[20] It discourages standing pat, and celebrates vision and imagination. If we didn't believe these things, we wouldn't buy into institutional fads.

SOCIAL NETWORKS
FOR SPREADING NOVELTIES

But beliefs alone cannot explain institutional fads. Novelties emerge and spread within particular social contexts. Believing in progress might make people willing to consider a new way to teach kids to read, but there also need to be social networks through which news of this innovative teaching method can spread. American institutions tend to be organized in two ways that particularly encourage the spread of novelties.

Decentralization

First, American institutions tend to be decentralized; that is, they consist of many relatively autonomous organizations. Consider the schools that those 4 million first-graders will enter next fall. In some countries, all schools are subunits of a national educational bureaucracy. American education, in contrast, is organized around local school districts, which range from tiny rural districts containing one small school to huge, urban districts with hundreds of schools.[21] While state boards of education provide some oversight, each school district—and there are over 15,000 nationwide—has considerable freedom in deciding how its students will be taught. Similarly, there are thousands of independent hospitals and clinics, colleges and universities, and corporations. In our society, institutions tend to consist of many organizations that have a good deal of autonomy in choosing how they will operate.[22]

This decentralization creates many possible settings where novelties might be adopted. In centralized institutions, decisions tend to be made by a few key people who set all policies; centralization means that novelties have a hard time spreading unless they first gain acceptance at the top. In contrast, decentralization allows novelties to begin pretty much anywhere in the institution. Someone with a new method of teaching reading can approach 15,000 different school districts that might adopt the method. Theoretically, if some teacher in a small rural school found a better way of teaching reading, that method could spread to all American schools through the process of diffusion. Decentralization suggests that organizations can choose how they will operate; it implies that there might be great variation among the organizations within a given institution. In practice, however, we know that most institutions' organizations tend to conform, to resemble one another, so that schools in different districts aren't all that different.[23] To account for this conformity, we need to consider the links among an institution's organizations.

Connections

Decentralization allows for lots of points in an institution where a novelty might catch on, but how do such innovations spread? They spread via social networks, the webs of contacts that connect people in different organizations to one another. (Chapters 3 and 4 will discuss these ties in more detail; here, I merely want to note some of the ways people can be connected.) Obviously, individuals who belong to the same organization have ties to one another. It is easy to understand how one teacher's success with a new way of teaching reading might spread to other teachers in the same school. After all, those teachers eat lunch together and see one another in the teachers' lounge; they have lots of opportunities to exchange news. But how does news flow from one organization to the next?

Institutions have social networks that span organizations. Some of these involve formal ties; there are, for instance, professional associations for teachers—and for principals and district supervisors—that hold annual meetings to bring people from different organizations together and thus serve to spread news about what's happening across the institution. Other links are informal, such as friendships among teachers who received their training at the same university, went on to teach at different schools, but still keep in touch. When you start to think about it, there are all sorts of connections that tie people within institutions to one another.[24]

There are also people who specialize in spreading information. The most obvious are those who work in various news media. We tend to focus on the big, prominent media—the television networks, or major newspapers and magazines. But take a moment to appreciate the full range of media, many of them directed toward—and of interest only to—people in particular institutions: all the trade publications and professional journals, the countless newsletters, the Web sites and Internet discussion groups. All of these media exist to spread news, to keep people posted about what's happening. A similar role is played by the various consultants who move from one organization to another, offering advice on better ways to do things. Some of these connections span the gaps between institutions, as when doctors or educators who read the *Wall Street Journal* learn about developments in business, and think about how those changes might improve hospitals or schools.

Note that these networks can cross national—as well as organizational and institutional—boundaries. Professional associations, friendship networks, and media coverage connect people in different countries. So does the spread of multinational organizations; the process of globalization makes it increasingly easy for innovations to spread widely.[25]

All these networks of links provide the routes along which novelties can diffuse; the more connections, the easier it is for people in a given institution to learn about—and adopt—innovations. These ties explain why even people in the most isolated organizations in decentralized institutions can learn about novelties—and often wind up adopting the same ones, so that an institution's organizations come to resemble one another. Of course, when different organizations, institutions, or indeed societies adopt an innovation, they often alter it to fit their particular needs, so that novelties morph into new forms even as they spread.[26]

A FOUNDATION FOR FADS

Thus, our culture and society provide a context for institutional fads—a foundation upon which they can be built and spread. Our beliefs in progress, perfectibility, revolution, and rationality reflect our experiences with change, and make us more willing to consider new ideas. Our institutions, by combining decentralization with dense social networks, invite innovations and make it easy for them to spread. We are ready—culturally programmed and structurally organized—to consider, and perhaps adopt, new ideas.

We shouldn't take this for granted. It is easy to point to cultures that are far less welcoming of change—cultures, governed by traditions, rituals, or taboos, that approach change with greater suspicion. Such cultures value what they have, and doubt that they need anything else. They discourage innovation, particularly when it comes from the young (because in voicing new ideas they show disrespect for their elders), women (who should know their place), or foreigners (whose inferior ways can only contaminate and damage the social order). Such change-resistant cultures are much less susceptible to institutional fads.[27]

In contrast, our society is relatively willing to embrace change, and we believe that our history demonstrates that this openness to innovations is a good idea. For this reason, it is a mistake to characterize institutional fads as irrational, as some sort of mass insanity that sweeps aside good sense. Institutions that adopt novelties do so not out of deranged passion but in the conviction that they should be willing to improve their performance by try-ing something new.

All this helps explain the illusion of diffusion described in the first chapter. Novelties—such as a new approach to teaching first-graders to read—have their proponents. They—and the audiences they seek to persuade—believe in change, progress, perfectibility, and rationality. When people tie their hopes to some new idea, it is easy for them to confidently reject sugges-tions that this change will simply prove to be a fad. The next chapter explores these proponents' views. While this is a book about changes that turn out to be short-lived fads, it is important to remember that when these ideas are being introduced and are spreading, many people believe that the changes will be significant and lasting. Thus, I will often speak of these new ideas as innovations or novelties rather than as fads, because that is how they are experienced as the fad cycle begins.

3

The Fad Cycle

Emerging

━━━━━━━

Recent management fads offer a clear example of our culture's fascination with perfection. They urge businesses to improve *quality:* that is, to cut costs through more perfect performance by making fewer errors in producing goods and serving customers. In the early 1980s, firms were supposed to organize *quality circles* in which workers and managers could discuss ways to improve quality. As enthusiasm for quality circles faded, *Total Quality Management* appeared on the scene; here the pursuit of quality was supposed to govern all the firm's activities. Yet already by 1992, *Newsweek* was reporting that "TQM . . . has stumbled badly over its early, inflated expectations." TQM's decline set the stage for a rising new scheme for achieving quality—*business process re-engineering,* or BPR. A 1993 *Fortune* cover story ("Reengineering: The Hot New Managing Tool") insisted that BPR was no fad: "Business process reengineering is the hottest trend in management. . . . The telltales of faddishness are fluttering. . . . Get ready for the backlash, right? Wrong. Reengineering is for real." Except that only two years later, the *Boston Globe* declared: "Re-engineering is losing its luster"; according to one consultant,

"Reengineering is a fad."[1] (That BPR was blamed for heavily publicized decisions to lay off thousands of workers through unpopular downsizing strategies may have helped account for its speedy fall from grace.) But even as corporations abandoned their commitments to BPR, businesses began seizing on *Six Sigma*—a new program that promised to guide managers in achieving quality.

Thus, the quality circle begat TQM, and TQM begat BPR, and BPR begat Six Sigma. Each program arrived on the scene bright with promise: forget those old, ineffective quality programs; this one is the real deal:

DILBERT © Scott Adams / Dist. by United Feature Syndicate, Inc.

Corporations adopted each new program (often with great fanfare), trained their managers in its precepts, and then (usually quietly) abandoned it when the results proved disappointing. The pattern illustrates the life cycle of institutional fads. It is a process with three stages—what we'll call *emerging*, *surging*, and *purging*. This chapter—and the two that follow—will examine the stages in that cycle: here, we will consider how institutional fads emerge; chapter 4 will explore their surging popularity; and chapter 5 will address purging—their eventual collapse.

To explore how people are affected during these three stages, each chapter will describe the experiences of an imaginary figure—someone operating within a fad-prone institution—who can help us understand how people relate to institutional fads. This chapter's figure will be a physician: we'll call him Dr. Michael. (We could just have easily picked someone in another institution—a teacher, a corporate executive, or whatever—to illustrate the same principles.) But thinking about some problems Dr. Michael faces can help us see how and why innovations emerge within not just medicine but other institutions as well. We begin with every institutional fad's promise—to solve a problem.

THE BASIC REQUIREMENT: A GOOD STORY

Every institutional fad offers the prospect of progress—it proposes to make things better by solving some problem that bedevils the people involved in an institution. Fads such as hula hoops don't have to make sense; they can spread simply because they seem different and amusing. But institutional fads spread among smart people who need to believe that adopting this change is sensible, that it promises improvement. Such promises involve a two-part story: there is (1) a problem, and (2) a solution.

Problems

Let's begin with a situation facing this chapter's imaginary figure, Dr. Michael. Think of Dr. Michael as a good doctor, someone who does his best to cure his patients' illnesses. Now imagine that two sick patients turn up in his office. The first has what we might describe as a perfect disease—let's call it *unambiguitis*. This disease—serious, debilitating, maybe even life-threatening—is easily identified by the combination of symptoms A, B, and C: medical science has established that every person with that combination of symptoms has unambiguitis, and everyone with the disease displays those symptoms. Further, this disease is well understood; medical researchers have established its cause (say, some particular germ) and they understand the process by which that germ causes those symptoms. Finally, this is a perfect disease because it has a perfect treatment—people suffering from unambiguitis are to be given Pill Q; in every instance, Pill Q, which is readily available, will cure unambiguitis completely, inexpensively, and without complications or side effects. In other words, we can call unambiguitis a perfect disease because it is well understood, easily diagnosed, and easily cured—it is difficult to see how medicine could improve on its treatment of this disorder. Unambiguitis poses no problems for Dr. Michael.

In contrast, Dr. Michael's second patient poses a much tougher problem, even though the patient's medical condition is not life-threatening. This patient reports feeling lousy and wants Dr. Michael to do something, to cure the illness. However, the patient's symptoms don't lend themselves to a clear diagnosis; they include feeling tired and listless; having trouble sleeping; feeling stiff and sore; having headaches, a sore throat, and swollen glands; running a slight fever; and so on. One problem for Dr. Michael is that these symptoms are ambiguous, in that they don't point clearly and definitively to a particular disorder— they might be associated with various diseases, so Dr. Michael must conduct tests to rule out possible diagnoses. In the end, all the tests are inconclusive, and Dr. Michael cannot specify exactly which disease is afflicting the patient. Nor is there a generally agreed-on, consistently successful treatment that is known to resolve this constellation of symptoms. Although the patient feels sick and has come for help, Dr. Michael is unable to provide either a specific diagnosis or an effective treatment.

This is not a fanciful problem—real doctors encounter real patients with such complaints. Over the years, the medical literature has featured various attempts to name the disease implicated in these symptoms, using such labels as *atypical poliomyelitis, myalgic encephalitis*, and—most recently—*chronic fatigue syndrome* and *fibromyalgia syndrome;* but these diagnoses are widely seen as unsatisfactory, in that the symptoms are not definitive, there is no general agreement regarding their cause (or even whether they should be understood as biological or as psychological in origin), nor is there a generally effective treatment.[2] Patients with these symptoms feel ill, and they don't want to be told that they're suffering from a psychiatric problem; they want their doctors to make them well. Confronted with such cases, Dr. Michael and his colleagues are likely to feel understandably discouraged—in spite of their best efforts, they can't do all that much to help patients with these symptoms. This disease poses an apparently intractable problem, one that frustrates both Dr. Michael and his patient.

There is a great gulf between unambiguitis (well understood and easily controlled) and the conditions recently termed chronic fatigue syndrome and fibromyalgia syndrome (imperfectly understood and difficult to treat). The former represents an ideal—a case in which the institution of medicine works well; the latter reveal lots of room for improvement. And it is identifying such shortcomings—the problems facing institutions and the people who work in them—that provides the first part of every institutional fad's story.[3]

Note that most institutions have familiar problems; in many cases these problems seem inevitable, even inherent in the institution itself. For example, the logic of capitalism ensures that businesses can never be satisfied with their performance; they must always seek lower costs and higher profits. Schools will always want to teach more, scientists will inevitably seek to do more research to increase what is understood about the world, and so on. There are always gaps between where we are and where we'd like to be. This means that people like Dr. Michael, who work in institutions, know that they face problems, that things could be better.[4]

There are various ways to identify and package problems, to present them in the stories that promote institutional fads.[5]

- There may be an announcement of a brand-new problem— perhaps something that has never before occurred (think of all of the new problems made possible by the development of the Internet, such as Internet addiction or Internet stalking).

- Or perhaps the problem has been around but people have ignored it, and they are only now becoming aware of and drawing attention to it (thus, people began using the term *sexism* in the early 1970s, although everyone understood that treating the sexes differently had a very long history).

- Or maybe something didn't used to be considered a big problem, but the world has changed, and now people claim that a crisis looms (for example, a globalizing economy confronts once-dominant American industries with overseas competition, or modern air travel means that the Ebola virus and other diseases once confined to remote corners of the world have the capacity to spread quickly and widely).

- In still other cases, the problem is understood to be an old one, but it is being given a new name (say, chronic fatigue syndrome instead of myalgic encephalitis); sometimes, the old name may itself be considered part of the problem because it carries negative connotations (so that educators who once described students as *culturally deprived*—a term originally intended as a polite, professional label for the special problems facing children growing up in poverty— began recognizing that that label had unfavorable connotations, and began substituting another—*at risk*).[6]

- Or people may acknowledge that the problem is familiar, of long standing, but they may claim to have identified a new cause—or some other new aspect—of it.

There are many possible ways to characterize problems, but the point should be clear: every institutional fad begins with a story about something that is wrong, some shortcoming, some need for improvement.

Solutions

Of course, it is not enough to pose a problem; an institutional fad's story must also offer a solution. The solution is proposed as a way of fixing whatever is wrong. Just as problems can take many forms, so can solutions. But several themes run through most solutions.

Novelty

First, solutions promise change. Whatever we've been doing hasn't been working (we know that, because we have a problem);

therefore we need to try something else.[7] The solution promises a break from the past, a commitment to do something new and different.[8] Actually, it need not be all that new—one popular type of solution is to call for reviving some past practice that, its promoters argue, has (unwisely) fallen out of favor. Thus, advocates of using phonics to teach reading insist that educators were foolish to abandon this tried-and-true method, that the difficulty experienced by today's children in learning to read is caused by the ineffective methods that replaced phonics, and that schools ought to return to what works.[9] In any case, virtually all institutional fad stories begin by arguing that what we've been doing hasn't solved the problem, so let's do something else.

Explanation

Clearly, just calling for change is not enough. Promoting a solution usually requires a rationale, an understandable explanation for why this particular solution promises to work better. Thus, proponents of phonics insist that it teaches children how to sound out unfamiliar words, giving them the basic tools to decipher most words, while advocates of the chronic fatigue syndrome diagnosis argue that patients' various symptoms are caused by a virus (and that viewing the disease in this way will help doctors devise different, more effective treatments). Because our culture sees progress as linked to rationality, it is important to explain the logic behind a proposed change. Explanations give people a reason to adopt the new solution. Note that most people probably can't fully understand the explanation, but they are comforted that there is one—they can tell themselves that this innovation makes sense because experts now understand the problem. The most attractive explanations therefore tend to be simple—they identify some single, easily understood cause, some key factor, so that people can convince themselves that they understand the basic problem and its solution.[10]

Evidence

Evidence bolsters the explanation—it supports the claim that *this* is the solution to the problem. Evidence can come in many forms, but anecdotes—success stories—are far and away the most common: this child learned to read using phonics; that doctor seems to be having success treating patients with chronic fatigue syndrome; company X's profits rose after it adopted our new management technique.[11]

Such parables fall far short of scientific proof. For scientists, controlled experiments that have been replicated set the "gold standard" for proof, but that sort of solid evidence is rarely available when a novel solution is first proposed. Scientists have learned that shortcutting this research process—jumping to conclusions before gathering sufficient evidence to check whether they are right—leads to embarrassment, as in the cold fusion mess described in chapter 1.[12]

But compiling a convincing mass of experimental evidence takes a great deal of both time and money (think of the years and huge investments needed to gain approval to market a new prescription drug). Sure, it would be nice to have more evidence, but in the meantime we know our institution faces problems—patients feel sick, kids fall behind grade level, and so on—and this new solution certainly seems promising, because we can point to examples of its apparently working. And we suspect that others are climbing aboard the bandwagon. If we delay adopting this innovation until there is more evidence, while our competitors adopt it now, they could get the jump on us. Can we really afford to wait for more evidence?[13]

Mystery

At the same time that the solution is promoted as rational and backed by evidence, it may simultaneously be assigned mysterious, even mystical properties. Analysts of management fads speak of them being promoted by "management gurus" and "organizational witchdoctors."[14] While tinged with irony, these terms are more respectful than skeptical; in particular, the business press bestows the label *guru* freely—and positively—"to indicate a far-sighted and visionary individual" who might reveal "hidden knowledge or secrets."[15] Gurus have disciples, acolytes, and devotees, who buy into a message delivered in books and—most powerfully—in performances dispensed in person at workshops and conferences, or via videos.[16] In these highly emotional presentations, "the message is posed in riddles, dilemmas, mysteriously gained insights."[17] This quality of mystery helps trump those complainers who carp about insufficient evidence—what is required is a willingness to believe, to make a leap of faith, to follow a visionary ideal. Again, what we're doing now isn't working—we still have problems—and here's the solution, if only we aren't afraid to believe in it, so let's take the risk.

Breadth

One of the most interesting features of the solutions promised by institutional fads is their flexibility or breadth. Promoters often claim that a single solution has the power to resolve multiple problems. Consider, for example, the 1990s calls to require public school students to wear uniforms. Why? Because uniforms promised to resolve a host of problems facing parents and schools. Uniforms would be cheaper for parents than buying the designer outfits marketed for children, and they would minimize resentments felt by students envious of their classmates' more expensive and more stylish costumes. Uniforms could control the potential display of gang colors, and ensure that students would not wear inappropriate or provocative clothing that might disrupt learning. Proponents insisted that schools that required uniforms had fewer discipline problems and higher academic performance.[18] School uniforms, then, became a panacea. It hardly mattered what you considered to be the key problem facing schools; whatever the trouble might be, school uniforms offered the solution. Clearly, a solution's potential appeal is increased if it promises to solve several problems rather than just one. Just as people with problems are looking for solutions, so those who think they have solutions search for multiple problems they might solve.[19]

Breadth can be enhanced by describing the solution in abstract terms. Rather than presenting a solution to address, say, inventory-control problems in the widget industry, why not speak in terms of "managing"? After all, managing is required not just in every business but in schools, hospitals, government agencies—in all sorts of organizations. Similarly, solutions might involve "learning," "excellence," "quality," "efficiency," or other abstractions that can be interpreted as applicable in many settings, in many institutions, and in many countries, thereby vastly enlarging the prospective market for the solution[20] (see box on p. 56). If the language is sufficiently general, who can challenge its applicability?

One analyst observes: "management's gurus . . . work hard to divest themselves of the fetters of the physical world—the ties of

---

ADMINISTRATION BABBLE

Generalities and Jargon Can Overpower Specifics

How "We" Will Achieve These Goals

"Collaborative Effort and Interface"

and

"A Systematic Comprehensive Approach"

through

"Focused and Action-Oriented Dialogues"

– PowerPoint slide from a presentation by a university administrator

---

time and space; the idiosyncrasies of local institutions; and the complexities and ambiguities of organizational performance, which might otherwise restrict international market opportunities."[21] As a result, solutions may mean different things to different people: adopters may be drawn to different aspects of a solution, and even individuals within a particular organization may have very different understandings of just what the solution involves and how it ought to be implemented. Yet these differences often can be obscured when all profess allegiance to the solution's general principles.[22] In particular, advocates generally downplay any potential trade-offs: the advantages of adopting the innovation are emphasized, while any prospective costs or disadvantages tend to be ignored.[23]

Breadth may take other forms, such as ideological breadth. Consider the early 1990s wave of enthusiasm for boot camps— correctional institutions for young offenders modeled on military training. Boot camps appealed both to conservatives (who favored "getting tough" with these youths, to "teach them some discipline") and to liberals (who may have been attracted by the metaphor of the boot camp as training for entry into a respectable career, as a way to reform rather than merely punish). Note that school uniforms also appealed to liberals (who saw them as a way of minimizing social class distinctions and thereby improving students' self-esteem), as well as conservatives (who emphasized uniforms' role in making schools disciplined, orderly, and focused on academics).[24] While it isn't essential that an institutional fad appeal to the full ideological spectrum, such broad appeal is obviously an advantage, in that it attracts more potential adherents, and any opposition to the innovation is less likely to be organized.[25] Once again, the more people who can find something to like about a solution, the easier it is to find folks willing to buy into the innovation. As a result, people promoting a novelty are encouraged to make expansive promises regarding its worth.

A Recipe

Although solutions tend to be abstract rather than specific, they often feature memorable elements that seem to make the solution easier to apply. Constituting a sort of prepackaged recipe for success, these include aphorisms, slogans, lists, principles, steps to be taken, and other guidelines to applying the solution.[26] Such condensed bits of wisdom can be displayed on PowerPoint slides, screen savers, posters, T-shirts, and other media suitable for displaying thought bites. Often, the new solution requires adopting a new vocabulary with its own jargon, abbreviations, buzzwords, and doublespeak—talking the talk apparently being the first step toward walking the walk.[27] Being able to express yourself in the new language and apply the new concepts signals that you have bought into the solution.

Status

It also helps if a solution has connotations of high status. The news that this solution has been endorsed by researchers at a prominent university, by a well-known corporation, or by an athletic coach with a winning record encourages people to emulate those they admire by adopting the solution their heroes favor.[28] A complex society offers many arenas within which people can achieve visibility, so that it is not all that difficult to link a solution to someone with some sort of high prestige. The solution's popularity can itself suggest high status; its promoter can be hailed as a best-selling author, popular inspirational speaker, or well-known consultant—the promoter's very claim to have gained lots of people's attention proves that others should start listening. While status might not seem to be an essential element for a solution, it is, as we will see, extremely important in fostering the spread of institutional fads.

When packaged together, these elements—novelty, explanation, evidence, mystery, breadth, a recipe, and status—present the solution as a plausible, promising way for dealing with what has been an intractable problem. Such ideas have the potential to become institutional fads. But, of course, ideas are not enough. The fad also needs a way to spread.

NETWORKS AND NOVELTIES

To understand how institutional fads spread, we need to think about social networks, the connections among people. Let's return to Dr. Michael. As a physician, he belongs to several complex social networks: Dr. Michael has firsthand contacts with other doctors in clinics and hospitals; he belongs to professional associations for physicians, including organizations just for doctors in his specialty; he receives journals, newsletters, and other publications aimed at physicians like himself; he attends professional conferences and workshops; and he may even belong to e-mail lists that bring him into electronic contact with his peers. The very existence of these professional venues is justified by their ability to help doctors like Dr. Michael keep up with what's happening in medicine, and particularly with those developments that might affect his practice. That is, everyone assumes that modern medicine will feature new diagnoses, as well as new treatments, drugs, devices, and techniques, and that part of being a good, professional physician is staying on top of these developments. Note that there are lots of folks—drug company representatives, the people who produce publications aimed at physicians, and so on—whose *jobs* are to keep Dr. Michael and his colleagues in the know.

In addition, Dr. Michael deals with patients who receive their own medical updates from conversations with friends, news reports, magazine articles, Internet searches, talk shows, "disease of the week" made-for-TV movies, and advertisements. Remember that in our culture, everyone—doctors and patients alike— anticipates that medicine will be changing, and for the better. The dense social networks that envelop medicine reinforce this impression by enabling medical news to spread rapidly.

And medicine is not unique. Every institution has parallel social networks that connect people who are involved in education, or business, or whatever. Some of these contacts involve personal, face-to-face links with people who know one another, work together, and may even be friends. But other ties are *mediated*. In contemporary society, most institutions have developed elaborate social networks built on associations, conferences, trade journals, and other mechanisms for exchanging news of interest. Consider that word: *news*. It conveys the importance of novelty, of change, of, well, what's *new*. In a culture that celebrates change and progress, we establish and maintain dense webs of institutional social ties because we expect there to be news; we assume things will change, and this assumption, in turn, creates its own demands for media that can tell us what's happening.

All of these media venues—from the humblest newsletter seeking material to fill the next issue to mass media with great prestige and vast audiences—need news to report. They are eager to locate what folks in the media call *content*, and many of the best stories involve bringing some innovation or novelty to the attention of their audiences. Obviously, the more interesting the news, the better. Old news is, as they say, stale; fresh information is highly valued. A report of big changes—of a possibly revolutionary discovery or a seemingly dramatic breakthrough—makes more compelling news than, say, information that researchers' replications have reaffirmed what most experts in the field were already thinking. That is why those dubious claims about cold fusion became a media sensation, even though the evidence on which they were based had not appeared in a reputable journal and proved unable to bear close inspection: the media saw cold fusion as a huge story about finding the secret to cheap energy—or at least it would have been huge, if only the researchers had turned out to be correct.

The media have, in short, a built-in bias in favor of novel

claims; claims of progress—particularly reports of dramatic developments—easily gain their attention. Moreover, the expansion of media coverage, particularly the emergence of such around-the-clock venues as the Internet and twenty-four-hour cable television networks devoted to news, business, and health, means that there is an insatiable media appetite for fresh stories. In a world hungry for novelty, it is a singularly unappealing innovation that cannot attract some attention.[29] In fact, the media's eagerness to report on the newest, most cutting-edge novelties leads to media coverage regularly preceding—and encouraging—widespread adoption of the innovation; by the time the novelty is actually spreading, the media already are looking for newer news to report.[30]

Because each institution has its own professional associations and media, it is considerably easier for novelties to spread within one institution than to cross the boundaries between institutions. Moreover, not all solutions will have cross-institutional appeal; physicians may be quite interested in chronic fatigue syndrome as a new diagnosis for patients who report feeling listless, but the new label isn't likely to offer much of a solution to problems recognized by, say, teachers or business executives. This is why it is important to emphasize a solution's breadth. The most successful institutional fads are framed as generalities—while interest in chronic fatigue syndrome is likely to be limited to doctors, every institution has problems that can be defined and addressed by innovations in learning or managing. This is also why individuals who connect two otherwise distinct networks, sometimes described as *weak ties* or *boundary spanners*, are so important.[31] A physician who also has friends in business can help spread news of medical innovations to the business world, and information about business innovations to medicine. And some general media, such as the *New York Times*, also carry sufficiently detailed reports of doings in particular institutions to frequently attract the attention of people in very different networks.

The networks within and among institutions help explain why organizations and institutions tend to resemble one another—that is, any given hospital tends to be organized along the lines of other hospitals, and the same can be said for schools, corporations, and so on.[32] Such likeness occurs for various reasons; for instance, laws may require the adoption of certain arrangements. But even without legal pressure, some organizations deliberately imitate what seems to be working elsewhere. Here, media reports play a key role in spreading the word about apparently effective innovations, thereby fostering such imitation. Institutional similarities also are fostered by professional networks that span particular organizations. Thus, a school district's financial officer is part of that district's social network, but he or she probably also belongs to one or more associations for financial officers in education, and returns from association meetings with ideas about how other districts are doing things. This sense that something is normative, that the way others are behaving is the way we ought to be doing things, can be very powerful.

While sociologists seem to imply that growing similarities among organizations involve the diffusion of enduring changes, it should be obvious that some of what gets copied will turn out to be short-lived enthusiasms—that is, institutional fads. Once again, it is important to appreciate the value of generalities. An innovation that is defined in very narrow, concrete terms (say, news that school districts may be able to take advantage of a particular accounting method) will probably not spread all that far. In contrast, vaguer, more abstract claims about managing change or discovering excellence have the potential to spread much further within and across institutions.[33]

Here, too, it helps to think about the importance of status. Individuals and organizations find it easier to emulate those they admire—high-status figures in their worlds. News that Top Ivy University or Supergoliath Corporation has adopted some new method is likely to impress those at lesser schools and companies. Similarly, whole institutions may look up to others. Academic administrators in higher education apparently worry that they aren't nearly as adept at facing management problems as their counterparts in the corporate world; they imagine corporate warriors handling tough, real-world challenges, in stark contrast to the protected ivory-tower existence of deans and provosts. Although it takes a little time for the word to reach academia, management methods that begin in the business world often get picked up by college and university administrators who want to imitate those they think of as real managers.[34] Similarly, the institutional practices in one country may be copied in another. Often American innovations spread to other countries (a common pattern with innovative management practices), but the diffusion sometimes occurs in the opposite direction.[35] Thus, during the late 1970s and early 1980s, panicky fears that American industry was being overtaken by Japanese competitors that were more efficient and better managed led to the importation of such Japanese management practices as quality circles. Of course, the reputations that convey status are not permanent; Americans' eagerness to emulate the Japanese diminished in the 1990s, after Japan's aptly named "bubble economy" burst.[36]

THE PROCESS OF EMERGENCE

It is all very well to say that cultural assumptions and social networks make institutional fads possible, but how do fads actually emerge? To understand this process, we need to consider both a cast of characters and a sequence of stages.

Actors and Innovation

Originators

Different sorts of people are involved in launching institutional fads. Most obviously, there must be originators: those who create some new idea or process that can be presented as the solution to some problem, that has the potential to transform and improve an institution. This innovation may not ensure perfection, but it promises a great advance toward that end. By adopting this innovation, businesses will become more profitable, organizations more efficient, education and medicine more effective—the particular goal depends on the institution, but the glorious promise of progress remains the same.

Originators come in all forms. Some are theorists or inventors, who devise some new idea and find satisfaction in this creativity. The creators may not themselves fully appreciate or be particularly interested in the broad practical potential of their innovation, or perhaps they don't know how to get the innovation adopted. Other originators are less naive; they set out to convince others that their novelty should spread. That is, they double as promoters.

Promoters

Promoters take on the task of disseminating the innovation. They may have a financial stake in its success, or they may be altruistic true believers who are convinced of the novelty's promise. Some are professional promoters: entrepreneurs and public-relations specialists are examples (I will have more to say about these folks below). Members of the media who publicize the innovation and report on its spread also play a role in promotion. In addition, anyone who adopts the novelty has the potential to become a promoter, simply by virtue of telling others about the innovation and encouraging them to adopt it, too.

Promotion can be turned into a lucrative career, as the gurus who promote management fads clearly demonstrate. The path to guruhood begins with writing a business book (which becomes the subject of its own publicity campaign, including book tours and reviews, author interviews, and feature stories in the business press). Ideally the book vaults onto the best-seller list (one scandal involved revelations that the authors of a business book—in collusion with their publisher—purchased thousands of copies of their own book in order to ensure that it qualified for the best-seller lists, as a means of drawing further attention to it).[37] Best-sellerdom in turn fosters far more lucrative opportunities for giving speeches at corporate gatherings and business conventions, and for consulting with different firms. The most successful gurus develop followings, so that they can bring out additional books that have the potential to keep the cycle going. Once again, the media play a vital role in the process of promoting these gurus' visibility.

Not all promoters occupy such glamorous positions. Ordinary individuals may promote novelties by becoming *internal champions* for particular changes. For example, one study found that schools were more likely to adopt a fluoride mouth rinse program (an inexpensive way to prevent cavities) when a school superintendent or some other figure insisted that it was important.[38] Note, too, that promoting a novelty can be a way to enhance prestige, either one's own or that of one's profession; thus, some nurses have promoted "healing touch" therapies that showcase nurses' important role in helping patients recover.[39]

Promoters do not always have a stake in particular innovations. The media, for instance, want to report on whatever is new. Similarly, professional associations provide settings where lots of innovations can be displayed to potential adopters; association meetings are places where promoters can display their wares, but also where colleagues can tell one another about their experiences with different novelties. The media and professional associations probably don't care which particular changes are in vogue, so long as there are some developments that keep people following the news and attending conferences.

Some promoters have the power to require adoptions of novelties; when the federal government mandates that states receiving federal funds for education must submit test data on student performance, most states—because they depend on receiving that money—are forced to comply (see box on p. 67).[40] Other promoters offer rewards for adopting innovations. For example, much scientific and medical research depends on grants from government agencies or foundations. An announcement that

---

MANDATED INNOVATION
Educators Respond

No Child Left Behind: The Football Version

1. All teams must make the state playoffs, and will win the championship. If a team does not win the championship, they will be held on probation until they are the champions, and coaches will be held accountable.

2. All kids will be expected to have the same football skills at the same time and in the same conditions. No exceptions will be made for interest in football, a desire to perform athletically, or genetic abilities or disabilities. ALL KIDS WILL PLAY FOOTBALL AT A PROFICIENT LEVEL.

3. Talented players will be asked to work out on their own without instruction. This is because the coaches will be using all their instructional time with athletes who aren't interested in football, have limited athletic ability or whose parents don't like football.

4. Games will be played year round, but statistics will only be kept in the 4th, 7th and 11th games.

5. This will create a New Age of Sports where every school is expected to have the same level of talent and all teams will reach the same minimal goals.

If no child gets ahead, then no child will be left behind.

— Photocopy circulating among teachers, 2005

---

some funding source has set aside millions for research on a particular topic is likely to cause many researchers to shift their focus in order to follow the money. Promoters' power, whether expressed as sticks or as carrots, pressures others to adopt the novelty. When bosses impose a new management scheme on their employees or the federal government offers grants to support community policing, those pressed to adopt the innovation may be suspicious or resentful rather than enthusiastic. In turn, their resistance may contribute to the fad's eventual demise.

Trendsetters

But promotion, by itself, cannot make an innovation spread successfully. People actually have to adopt the innovation. Key to this process are what studies of diffusion call *early adopters* or *opinion leaders*—those individuals who adopt the novelty first, when it is little known and little appreciated.[41] These are the *trendsetters*, who serve as examples for others. Trendsetters adopt novelties and set examples for followers who make the same choices, in part because those are the choices the trendsetters made.

Not everyone is cut out to be a trendsetter. Trendsetters need resources, particularly time and money. Time is necessary to discover, consider, and select novelties or innovations; people who are too busy to pay attention to what's new in the world aren't likely to lead the way in discovering some novelty. Trendsetters also need sufficient money to afford these choices; while trendsetters need not be rich, they need to be able to afford the costs of innovation—and they must be willing to spend their money on it. In addition, trendsetters need followers; others have to be aware of their activities, and be willing to follow their example.[42]

Some theorists assume that trendsetters must have high status, so that they will be imitated by subordinates trying to become more like their betters. We have already seen that high-status associations encourage others to adopt an innovation. However, contemporary society offers many examples of fashions originating among those of lower status—particularly youth cultures—and then spreading. What seems key to the process is that others look to the trendsetters as exemplary, because they are viewed either as knowledgeable individuals or as social types that represent creativity, adventurousness, or other social virtues that celebrate change.

Trendsetting can receive a boost from media coverage. Trendsetters' influence swells when the media promote their activities. Media coverage of early adopters can spread information about the emergence of a novelty far faster and more widely than word-of-mouth—or sight-of-eye—transmission. Sometimes, the media publicize new, trendsetting social types, such as hippies or yuppies. These news reports depict the costumes, language, and consumption habits of the new social type, simultaneously promoting the type as an alternative identity and the various elements of the new lifestyle as potentially adoptable innovations. (This distinction is important: relatively few people actually became hippies, but many wore their hair longer and copied other elements of hippie style.) The media portray these new social types as embodiments of social change—thereby both advertising the type's importance and reaffirming the media's ability to spot such developments within the society. In cases of institutional fads, trendsetters are often particular organizations—a business firm, a university, or a hospital—that report the successful adoption of some innovation. Again, it probably helps if these organizations already have high status; however, publicity about extraordinary successes may draw attention, regardless of which organizations claim these results.

By definition, most of those who adopt innovations are not trendsetters but people who follow the trendsetters' example. Trendsetters are experimenting, trying new things. Some of them may view novelty as a virtue in its own right; they want something *new*.[43] Their followers tend to be less adventurous; while they may find novelty appealing, they also will be influenced by the knowledge that the innovation has—or at least seems to have—worked for the trendsetters. Thus, their motivations tend to be more cautious and practical. (More will be said about these late adopters in chapter 4.)

This cast of characters—originators, promoters, and trendsetters—suggests various ways people can help launch innovations. The particulars vary from novelty to novelty, but the point is that usually different people need to become involved to get an innovation off the ground.

The Launch Sequence

An alternative way of thinking about the different sorts of people involved in launching some novelty is to consider the sequence of stages involved in this process.

The Original Idea

There is a natural tendency to get hung up on wondering about the origins of novelties. Who had the idea first? What were the circumstances that led to the discovery? Such questions lead to speculation about the nature of genius, creativity, and so on.

This line of inquiry is, for our purposes, a dead end. If we want to understand institutional fads, we need to think in terms of the larger process. Pick an institutional fad: say, Total Quality Management (TQM). TQM rose to great prominence in management circles in the late 1980s, then lost favor.[44] No doubt, during those heady days when TQM was the flavor of the month, people may have been intensely interested in just who originated the concept and how it came to pass. After all, we love success stories;

we've all heard how Thomas Edison's determination led to the invention of the lightbulb. But notice the difference: we're still using lightbulbs, so the Edison story remains interesting. In contrast, TQM is now just a fading memory, one more abandoned management fad. However brilliant the inventor of TQM may have seemed back in the day, that day is over, and most people no longer care.

Instead of worrying about who deserves the credit for a particular idea, we will be better off if we assume that there are, at any given time, lots of people with lots of new ideas. American culture's deep-seated belief in progress encourages folks to come up with these ideas, to think about ways of doing things differently, doing them better. The key question is not how someone came up with a particular idea but rather how that idea emerged from all of the available ideas to become a focus for attention.

Selection

Understanding an idea's emergence was the sociologist Herbert Blumer's point when he described the Parisian fashion industry. Blumer noted that each spring and fall, the haute couture designers presented hundreds of new creations, but interest inevitably coalesced around a handful of these designs. As the fashion world—the buyers, the fashion press, all the fashionistas— discussed the new offerings, they began to focus their attention on what people could agree were the most important designs. Blumer called this process *collective selection.*[45] There were lots of new designs, each with its own story of some inspiration that lay behind it, but knowing how a designer came to envision a particular design was less important than understanding how the fashion world came to agree that that design was stylish.

Selection is an interactive process with two key elements: news circulating about some novelty and people choosing to adopt that novelty. It has a chicken-or-the-egg quality: Does news spread because people are adopting some innovation? Or do people become interested in adopting the innovation because they hear that others have already done so? The answer is undoubtedly that both occur. Innovations—even institutional fads—typically start small. Somebody has an idea, and tries it out on a small scale—maybe by actually applying it in the real world (say, in a classroom, or with a couple of patients), or maybe just by writing down some thoughts. This originator tells others, who may decide to adopt the novelty. The process escalates: trendsetters begin adopting the innovation, and the number of promoters swells as the media begin noting the trend (typically, small media with specialized audiences report first, then the news reaches mainstream media with bigger, more general audiences). There is no single, standard path along which all innovations travel. Several things can happen at the same time—those who are already adopters talking to potential adopters, adopters coming to the attention of the media, media reports and other promoters alerting potential adopters to the novelty, and media reports coming to the attention of other media. At some point in this process, individuals such as Dr. Michael become aware that there is some innovation—such as a new diagnosis for patients who report feeling tired—and consider adopting it. The process is complicated and confusing, and its outcome is by no means certain.

We tend to look at this process backward, focusing on the triumphant finish rather than the shaky start. Asked to think of a management fad, we imagine something like Total Quality

Management—a highly successful program adopted (however briefly) by hundreds of corporations. We know about it precisely because it was once a big success. But at the beginning, TQM probably didn't look all that much different from other fresh approaches to management (let's call them Plan A, Plan B, and so on) that other people were promoting. For all sorts of reasons— maybe Plan A's originator was shy and unwilling to speak in public, people weren't sure how to pronounce the foreign words in Plan B's name, Plan C's originator got discouraged when a publisher turned down her manuscript, state legislators were thought sure to object to Plan D, and too many people just didn't believe Plan E would work—these rival schemes fell out of favor, even as TQM kept gaining more advocates. While TQM's success might seem inevitable, any institutional fad that rises to the top has benefited from all sorts of contingencies that blocked potential rivals.[46]

Research

It is these innovations that have succeeded in spreading that become the subject of research to test their effectiveness (that is, research designed to see whether the innovation actually works better than what it is intended to replace). This might seem surprising. We tend to think of researchers as uncovering knowledge; shouldn't their discoveries be the foundation for innovation? However logical this assumption might seem, it is generally wrong. Remember that the key evidence in promoting institutional fads tends to be anecdotal—this school saw violence drop after they adopted uniforms, that well-known corporation swears by TQM, and so on. Such examples seem like powerful evidence in the early stages when an innovation is getting off the ground—

we know it worked for someone! In general, novelties spread before there has been time to conduct careful experiments into the innovations' effectiveness.[47]

More sophisticated research tends to come later in the process, after an innovation has attracted enough adoptions and enough attention to draw the notice of researchers.[48] It was only after corporations began adopting TQM that researchers figured out they ought to study how well it worked. Note that the researchers may well assume that the innovation is effective, and therefore seek to measure how well—rather than whether—it works. Note, too, that the news that researchers have begun to study an innovation can serve as another sort of promotion; after all, isn't the researchers' move to study some novelty, their deeming it worthy of attention, evidence that there must be something to the innovation? But the process of designing a research project, collecting the data, interpreting those data, and presenting or publishing the results takes time—probably at least a few years. In contrast, popular media try to cover stories as they are happening, while the news is still hot. So it should be no surprise that while popular media coverage tends to coincide with (and is in fact an integral part of) the rise of institutional fads, research results often do not appear until late in the fad cycle, often after the institutional fad has begun to fade.

TOWARD INSTITUTIONAL FASHION?

Chapter 1 characterized fads as episodic, one-shot affairs, and argued that fashion involves systems for the regular production of novelties. Because institutional fads are posed as solutions to intractable problems, fads tend to recur in particular institutions:

educators are constantly reforming schools, business is always on the lookout for better ways of managing, and so on. At what point does it make sense to characterize such a series of fads as fashion?

Clearly, the production of management fads has begun to resemble a fashion industry. It is not difficult to understand why this institution might lead the way. Every business has its problems: it can always hope to improve, to become more profitable (and it always fears that things could get worse, that profits could decline). In large enterprises, the process of management—that is, keeping track of all the employees and making sure that they stay on track and do what they're supposed to do—poses constant headaches, so there are intractable problems in need of solutions. Note, too, that business is a very large, decentralized institution: it comprises many firms employing many, many people; each of those firms and many of the people within them are potential adopters of problem-solving innovations; and many businesses are profitable enough that they can afford to try something new.

At the same time, business has generated a huge, complex social network to provide institutional support. There is the business press, which consists of thousands of publications, ranging from trade periodicals narrowly aimed at people in particular industries to large, broad-based publications such as the *Wall Street Journal;* all of these seek to cover news of relevant developments. There are the business schools, which insist they provide the most up-to-date undergraduate and graduate training for business leaders. There are consulting firms, themselves in the business of providing advice to other businesses. There are book publishers that seek to serve the business market. There is,

---

MANAGEMENT FAD NUMEROLOGY

Ten X Force
Nine Stepping Stones to Building a Winning Organization
Eight Revolutionary Rules for Becoming a Powerful and
    Exhilarated Leader
Seven S Model
Six Sigma
Five Forces Model
Four Obsessions of an Extraordinary Executive
Three Insatiable Customer Demands
One-Minute Manager
Zero Defects

– Taken from various books and programs offering advice for managers
(apparently **Two** is unmanageable)

---

in short, a very elaborate network available to spread news about innovations.[49]

A new management fad often begins with a book that offers some more or less fresh take on management. The most successful books become best sellers, perhaps in part through lots of individual sales; but it is also possible to sell thousands of copies at once if some large firm decides to buy copies in bulk and distribute them to its employees. And a best seller can be just the beginning; the theme can be repackaged in audiotapes, videos, and presentations before corporations and conferences, as well as serving as the basis for lucrative consulting contracts. A particular management theme may become a familiar brand, with a distinctive design—logo, typeface, and colors—that can be featured on follow-up books, calendars, and other products.[50] A successful management fad can make many millions (see box above).

Promoters now take a highly calculated approach to this high-stakes game. Publishers hope to hit it big, to create a brand built around an author. In interviews with Timothy Clark and David Greatbatch, editors involved in trying to publish management best sellers acknowledged that "When you publish these books you have to work on the assumption that most of the people who buy it won't read it" and that "Most 'authors' can't or won't write."[51] How do you produce best-selling books without either readers or authors? The process begins with would-be gurus and editors considering possible themes: "Editors . . . were not seeking fully formed books that could be published with minimal copyediting but rather the glimmer of an idea that they believed could be shaped and packaged to appeal to a management audience, and to promote the author and their brand."[52] Ghostwriters then develop manuscripts derived from the chosen theme (some individuals have ghostwritten best-selling management books for different guru-authors). The "author" is valued less for any writing talent than for the ability to perform effectively in speeches before audiences and on the training videos that will follow the book's success.

The results of these calculated efforts to manufacture enthusiasm for "brands" of management philosophy are apparent when researchers try to measure the rise and fall of different concepts in the business press.[53] Charting the number of articles published each year in business periodicals about, say, TQM produces the standard fad graph (similar to those in chapter 1). But observers have noted a pattern: with each successive management fad, the peak is higher but the time between the fad's rise and fall is shorter (that is, the business press publishes more articles about each successive fad—but within a shorter period of time—than about its predecessor). Management fads are becoming more intense, but shorter-lived. Established gurus often lead the way, abandoning a theme from an older best seller that is losing its influence in favor of introducing a new book with a new theme in hopes of recapturing their audience.[54]

In this case, the distinction between fad and fashion begins to blur. Some publishers, management gurus, and consulting firms seek to routinize enthusiasm for new management concepts— they are trying to establish what they are doing as a fashion industry, analogous to the production of hit movies or hot clothing designs. (The authors and publishers of books about diets, parenting, and other self-help topics display some of the same patterns.) However, the contours along which management (or diet, parenting, etc.) fads rise and fall are not yet so systematic that they require being labeled fashion (for example, there is nothing equivalent to the haute couture world's intense focus on the designers' fall and spring shows).

There is another problem. Audiences for fashion industries are not naive; they understand that styles change, and that they need to keep up. People who hope to dress in style expect to buy new clothes long before they wear out their old outfits. Media coverage openly acknowledges the flow of fashion—it is fun to learn about what designers or film studios have planned for the following season, to anticipate what might be next.

In contrast, institutional fads are promoted as serious, as real solutions to real problems. Dr. Michael (and his patients) don't want a diagnosis of the month, they want useful knowledge that will really cure disease. Similarly, when a corporation spends millions to retrain its employees to adopt a particular management plan, they presumably expect to register real gains in profits and not just experience the excited thrill of feeling they're in vogue.

It may be very well for editors to acknowledge in private that they make calculated efforts to assemble management philosophies as packages or brands—every activity has its backstage secrets.[55] But the audience—the potential adopters—doesn't want to know about these manipulations. They need to believe that this innovation represents progress, not just some trivial shift in styles: they need that illusion of diffusion. For it is their enthusiasm that causes institutional fads to surge.

4

The Fad Cycle

Surging

────────────

Consider low-carb eating—our new millennium's first big dietary enthusiasm. Its proponents promised that avoiding carbohydrates could lead to weight loss, as well as better sex and longer
life—our culture's lifestyle trifecta. Sure, we know better: our
heads may tell us that we need to eat less and exercise more in
order to lose weight. Still, our hearts can be swayed by claims that
the real secret to happiness lies in following some special diet.

Demonizing carbohydrates was not new: *Dr. Atkins' Diet Revolution* first topped the best-seller lists in 1973. But the new century
brought a revived wave of enthusiasm: new best sellers (such as
The South Beach Diet), reports that some researchers thought there
might be benefits to low-carb eating, proponents' bold declara-
tions that the new diet was here to stay, the food industry's eager
response (marketing beers and hamburgers with fewer carbohydrates), and countless conversations among ordinary people
weighing the merits of carb consumption. By 2004, nearly a tenth
of Americans claimed to be paying attention to their carb intake.[1]

Dieters—even those who have been disappointed by earlier
schemes—can get caught up in the promises of a new eating sys-

tem. Maybe this time will be different, they hope. Maybe this plan will work. And they climb aboard the bandwagon.

While we might like to imagine that science, with its emphasis on the careful evaluation of evidence, should be immune to fads, scientists also succumb to short-term enthusiasms. Take the notion of sustainable development, which swept through several scientific specialties in the 1990s. Agricultural scientists first used the concept of *sustainability* to refer to methods for managing natural resources, such as fish or soil. The term morphed into *sustainable development*, a notion that linked sustainability to the political goal of reducing inequality. The new term spread into various disciplines, where it took on "widely different meanings and usages at different time periods"; it became "a flag around which different constituencies [could] rally," "a 'hip' expression, part of the culture of granting agencies."[2] As such, it appeared in hundreds of articles published in scientific journals but soon fell out of favor, as attention shifted to other ideas. Once a sparkling term that might catch the eye of foundation officers and journal editors, sustainable development had become tarnished through overuse. Ahh, but when it was in vogue, the idea seemed exciting—a scholarly equivalent of low-carb eating.

After an institutional fad has run its course, people often have trouble explaining just what happened, and why. This is especially true of those who were not themselves caught up in the short-term enthusiasm. It is easy for someone who stood on the sidelines to ask why those supposedly smart people bought into that silly idea. What possessed them? Why did they waste their time, money, and energy on something they would soon abandon? It seems so crazy.

Attributing fads to craziness, to some sort of irrational impulse, is a tidy way of explaining puzzling behavior ("Most people behave rationally most of the time, but sometimes folks go a little nuts"). But there are at least two problems with such dismissals of faddish behavior. First, the same institutions experience one fad after another—just as diet fads spread through the general population, so business leaders adopt management fads, schools run through educational fads, and so on. Are those serious, rational institutions really prone to repeated fits of insanity? Why don't they learn from their past mistakes? Second, people in the process of adopting institutional fads don't think that they're being silly or crazy. They may suffer from the illusion of diffusion, but they think they're being smart. This chapter investigates the reasons that people in institutions decide to adopt novelties.

While the emergence of institutional fads can be a tentative and uncertain process, surging—the second stage of the fad's life cycle—often seems exuberant, exciting. Surging is the period when a fad's popularity grows most rapidly, when lots of people adopt the novelty. This chapter looks at three topics: it begins by exploring this exuberance and other emotional aspects of surging; then it considers some of the more calculated reasoning favored by those adopting innovations; and, finally, it examines those who are slow to adopt, including those who simply refuse to go along with the new trend.

THE JOYS OF JOINING

We need to remember that fads—even institutional fads promising solutions to serious problems—can be fun. When people are aware that an innovation is spreading, they often feel excited.

There is a widespread sense that being part of a big, important change has something thrilling, even joyful about it. Consider, for example, bull markets, when speculators rush to buy stocks, and prices spike. While we don't usually think of bull markets as fads, the two phenomena are similar, in that both are short-lived enthusiasms. And though economic theory depicts markets as rational arenas, economists often abandon the language of rationality and dismal science when describing bull markets and revert to speaking of emotion: John Kenneth Galbraith talks of "financial euphoria," Federal Reserve Board chair Alan Greenspan memorably characterized the 1990s boom as "irrational exuberance," and others use such terms as *manias, bubbles, crazes,* or *sprees.*[3] These episodes pose a problem for economic theories premised on actors making optimal, rational decisions, for investors in booms eagerly pay prices that turn out to be unrealistically high. The speculative bubble inevitably bursts, and a bear market drives prices back down, leaving many investors with great losses. Presumably they did not intend to lose their shirts. Is emotionalism somehow at fault?

Similarly, studies of social movements speak of *surges* or *soaring,* when people are enlisting in the cause and there is great optimism that the movement will succeed. Or consider the term *momentum,* used to characterize situations in which people feel that events—such as a sports team's scoring drive during a game—are flowing in a particular direction and cannot be halted.[4]

Stock bubbles, social movement surges, and momentum are all terms that seek to convey the emotional intensity of being caught up in change. The spread of innovations leads to similar emotional reactions, particularly as people become aware that

---

OFFICE FOLKLORE VIEWS THE EXCITEMENT OF INNOVATION

Getting Things Done around Here Is Like Mating Elephants

1. It's done at a high level.
2. It's accomplished with a lot of roaring and screaming.
3. AND it takes two years to get any results!!!!!!!

—In circulation since at least the 1970s

Source: Dundes and Pagter (1987: 103).

---

more and more folks are becoming adopters. I use the word *surging* to highlight these emotions, which have several sources.

First, promoters often deliberately seek to arouse enthusiasm and excitement among adopters and prospective adopters. A management guru's most important talent is to be an effective performer in presentations both before live crowds and on video.[5] These performances involve playing to the audience's various emotions, getting them to laugh, feel attached to the guru, worry about the threats posed by competing firms, yet anticipate the brighter future promised by the innovation. Promoters hold rallies, display posters and banners, and distribute T-shirts, buttons, and other knickknacks bearing distinctive logos and slogans. These trinkets not only enable adopters to affirm their commitment to the innovation but also help display the growing bandwagon to potential adopters. Getting people emotionally aroused makes it more likely they will adopt the novelty. In other words, some of the emotion of surging is a product of calculated efforts to excite lots of people about becoming adopters (see box above).

However, adopters also generate their own positive emotions. It is easy to find excitement in doing something different, if only because change breaks the boredom of routine.[6] This is particularly true if the change is seen as being part of progress, perhaps even of "history being made." Taking part in a new medical treatment or a new educational program breeds optimism—this may make things better, not just for those adopting now but for many others in the future, once the innovation spreads. There is pride in being a pioneer, one of the early adopters—the first kid on your block. These feelings are not limited to the institution's professionals—the doctors or the teachers adopting the change; they also can extend to those the institution serves, the patients or students who, to the degree that they are aware of the innovation, may find pride and hope in being the beneficiaries of progress.

This enthusiasm may cause a rush toward wholesale adoption. Thus, rather than gradually introducing a new program and testing its effectiveness—say, trying a new policy in one prison or a new program in one school and then carefully assessing how well it works—the leaders of the prison system or school district may decide to require everyone to adopt the innovation immediately. Such dramatic gestures may attract approving media coverage for the leaders' display of decisiveness.[7]

People also find comfort in being part of the in crowd, in joining with other adopters. To the degree that you admire the trendsetters, you will be pleased to join them. When you climb aboard the bandwagon, you reaffirm the choices of those who preceded you in adopting the novelty, and they, in turn, assure you that you've made the right decision. You're now an insider, a status that is part of the appeal of stylishness.[8] The feeling that you have made the right choice—whether eating the right diet or hiring the right corporate consultant—is not just personal ("It's the right choice for me") but also social ("Others will see that I've made the right choice, and they will admire me for being the kind of person who makes stylish choices; those who share my taste will welcome me as a comrade, while those who have not yet adopted the style will want to emulate me and become like me").[9]

In the case of institutional fads, there is the related comfort that if you and lots of other people have adopted this innovation, it is easier to believe that there must be something to it, and easier to deflect blame if it fails—after all, everyone else was doing the same thing.[10] Thanks to the complex networks of contacts and media that link an institution's members, people often know what others have been doing.[11] Thus, educators trying to establish statewide academic standards are aware of the sorts of standards already adopted in other states and don't want to be "out of step with national trends."[12] Remember, these are people making serious efforts to find solutions to what they view as real problems, so choosing to adopt an innovation is not a frivolous matter. It helps to be able to tell yourself that others have made the same choice, and it helps all the more if you admire some of those other adopters for their high status. Just as college students in the 1970s tended to streak when they knew that there had been streaking at a more prestigious campus nearby,[13] so knowing that a prominent corporate rival made big profits last year after it adopted a new management scheme makes your own choice of that program seem wiser.

In addition, adoption brings other, less positive emotions. The flip side of finding comfort in joining the crowd is the fear of being out of step, being left out. If all the other principals can share their schools' experiences with the newest educational reform, it is lonely to have to acknowledge that, well, no, your school hasn't made the shift. You don't want to find yourself in a situation in which everyone else is with it, but you're out of it. They'll be in fashion; you'll be old-fashioned. The pressure to conform—to avoid being isolated—grows as the innovation spreads, as the proportion who are adopters grows, and the number of you who still haven't made the shift shrinks. If you don't get on board, people may wonder about you or look down on you.[14]

Shame may be the least of it. Being slow to adopt can also arouse even more severe anxieties and fears. Management gurus often warn that the business world is becoming increasingly fast-paced and competitive, that those who stand pat risk being devoured by their competitors. They portray increasingly intense competition as *the* major problem facing business leaders, one that requires a new solution—the promoters' management scheme. Firms that refuse to change may—almost certainly *will*—wind up ruined. The cost of refusing to adopt can be presented as terribly high.

And looking down on non-adopters is yet another emotion aroused by adoption. Non-adopters have failed to do the right thing. They are ignoring the march of progress; they are not progressive. If they're our competitors, of course, their failure to adopt is good news for us—we will rise toward perfection, while they head the way of the dodo. But it is more frustrating when the resistance is internal. If our school or our company is supposed to be doing things differently, we don't want people within the organization refusing to go along and thereby subverting that progress. Such people are obstructionists who balk at getting with the program. They are reactionary, hidebound stick-in-the-muds. They're afraid of change, stuck in their rut, unwilling to try something new. They are cynical cheap-shot artists who can't recognize a good thing. There is, in short, a rather large vocabulary available for criticizing non-adopters. (These resisters have their own, different point of view, which I'll discuss later in this chapter.) Obviously, there is something to the non-adopters' fear of becoming socially isolated if they don't adopt the innovation— this is a real possibility, particularly as the ranks of adopters swell.

YOU CAN'T MOTIVATE ALL OF THE PEOPLE ALL OF THE TIME

MOTIVATION

IF A PRETTY POSTER AND A CUTE SAYING ARE ALL IT TAKES TO MOTIVATE YOU
YOU PROBABLY HAVE A VERY EASY JOB. THE KIND ROBOTS WILL BE DOING SOON.

Coupled with this frustration and anger with people who refuse to join the cause, adopters often also feel a sense of superiority because they have opportunities to exercise power. Once an organization's leaders have adopted some innovation, they may require their subordinates to get with the program—to attend training workshops, adopt the new lingo, and so on. Moreover, simply being in style makes it possible to look down on the less stylish. If you are convinced that you have made a wise and rational choice, those who fail to go along may increasingly strike you as foolish and irrational.[15] One of sociology's founders, Emile Durkheim, observed that the sense of cohesion and moral superiority felt by those who remain within the boundaries of their group's expectations depends, in part, on being able to criticize and exclude those who stand outside those boundaries.[16] In the same way, feeling superior requires being able to point to someone else who is inferior. If absolutely everyone adopts an innovation, it becomes much harder to feel that being an adopter boosts one's status.

These emotions, whether positive or negative, are felt by individuals. Institutional fads spread because individuals within organizations experience boredom, hope, pride, status seeking, status anxiety, and other feelings, and then decide to adopt the novelty that promises to improve things and make them feel better. As a result, members bring their organizations onto the bandwagon, and corporations, hospitals, and schools adopt innovations. Organizations experience two sorts of *bandwagon pressures*, both of which have their parallels among individuals: first, the knowledge that other organizations have adopted a novelty pulls us to think we ought to do the same; second, worries that our competitors may be taking advantage of the innovation to get the jump on us pushes us to act.[17] In other words, the logic and anxieties that shape organizational decisions parallel those that affect individuals' choices—which should not be that surprising, since any organization's decisions are ultimately made by the individuals who are its members.

CAREERISM AND OTHER CALCULATED RESPONSES

One problem with emphasizing the emotional satisfactions of adopting innovations is that we tend to think of emotion as the opposite of rationality. Thus, we might imagine that people who find emotional satisfaction in adopting a novelty are somehow not thinking through what they're doing. This would be a mistake. People who adopt innovations—including everything from fad diets to institutional fads—have their reasons; whatever emotions they are experiencing, they also are making calculated choices. Most obviously, of course, they see such innovations as promising progress, as solutions to pressing problems—people think adopting is the right thing for them to do. In addition, they may calculate that adoption offers advantages for them personally.

Consider the plight of Professor Alice, this chapter's imaginary figure; she has just received her Ph.D. and has been hired as an assistant professor of English literature by Thirdtier College. Professor Alice's tenured colleague, Professor Bertram, as well as her department chair, Dr. Charlotte, have warned her that she will not receive tenure and promotion to associate professor unless she publishes some articles in scholarly journals. As it happens, Professor Bertram and Dr. Charlotte actually haven't published all that much themselves, but standards have changed. Twenty-some years ago, when Professor Bertram and Dr. Charlotte joined Thirdtier's faculty, the college was pleased to hire faculty who held doctorates. But now, there are plenty of folks with Ph.D.s in English competing for jobs, and Daniel and Elaine—Thirdtier's dean and provost, respectively—have announced that all new faculty will be required to publish.

Professor Alice, then, has a problem. While she has to publish some sort of critical analysis of English literature, she faces an uncomfortable fact: Shakespeare won't be writing any more plays, and Jane Austen isn't going to publish any more novels. Scholarly journals won't publish anything that doesn't say something new—that doesn't, to use a phrase beloved by journal editors, "make a contribution." But there are already bookcases full of studies of Shakespeare and Jane Austen. What's left for Professor Alice to write about? What can she say that is new?

There are two well-worn solutions to this problem. The first is to criticize some less familiar work of literature, to "expand the canon" of analyzable works. Professor Alice could find some author whom previous scholars have ignored—perhaps someone whose race or gender or sexual orientation, she can argue, caused earlier scholars to overlook the literary value of the writer's work. In recent decades, many literary scholars have built their careers by calling attention to such long-neglected figures. This has been one of the attractions of studying multicultural literature—it opens whole continents of virtually unstudied literary works. Some literary scholars go further, identifying all manner of "texts" (say, the menus at popular fast-food restaurants) and insisting that these, too, can be subjected to analysis.

The second solution is to find some new approach, some new angle from which to view literature. New perspectives allow analysts to say something fresh—something editors will publish—about even the most familiar works, such as those by Shakespeare and Austen. Literature professors have been playing the new-perspectives game for many decades. Back when psychoanalysis was all the rage, there were literary interpretations based on Freud, of course, but also on the writings of Jung, Adler, and other lesser theorists of the unconscious. Similarly, Marx and other socialist thinkers inspired literary studies, as did various philosophical and intellectual movements—existentialism, structuralism, poststructuralism, postmodernism, and so on, and so forth. Professor Alice has seen an article in a newsmagazine about physicists studying something called "chaos theory." The name sounds promising. Professor Alice hasn't taken physics since high school, but she already has ideas for a title—something along the lines of "Kingdoms in Chaos: The Physics of Royal Courts in Shakespeare's Tragedies." Professor Alice's tenure is virtually assured.[18]

Professor Alice's tale illustrates how institutional fads (and, whatever its merits for physicists, in the hands of literature professors chaos theory can hardly be anything but a fad) may offer solutions to an individual's career problems (such as meeting Thirdtier's tenure requirements). Given our culture's fascination with change, individuals often find advantages in hooking their wagons to some rising enthusiasm. (This is probably one of the reasons that the concept of sustainable development spread as widely and rapidly as it did among scientists.) Becoming associated with a trendy novelty suggests to others that you are with it, on top of things, in the know, progressive, forward-looking—and all of those other clichés that assign approval to pioneers of novelty. Often, there are intimations of generational rivalries: those advocating changes are young lions, willing to stand up against the old guard. Institutional fads offer a rationale for turning the reins over to a new generation that is not mired in the past, one that welcomes the future.

Meanwhile, back at Thirdtier College, Provost Elaine realizes that the college's ten-year accreditation review by the Mid-Central Association of Higher Education is approaching. She's heard that sometime after Thirdtier's previous review, Mid-Central started insisting that colleges undergoing review submit "appraisal plans"—whatever those are. It looks like Thirdtier's going to need to develop an appraisal plan. Neither Provost Elaine nor Dean Daniel knows—or wants to know—anything about appraisal planning. They confer and appoint Professor Alice's colleague, Professor Bertram, to fill a new slot—Thirdtier's director of appraisal planning. (Note that just having a job with that title helps affirm Thirdtier's commitment to the new method.)[19]

Professor Bertram doesn't know anything about appraisal planning either, but he's happy to have a new job. Teaching his courses no longer seems as satisfying as it did when he started, and he isn't particularly interested in research; in fact, he's started to wonder whether he might not have what it takes to be a dean. Here's an opportunity to serve the Thirdtier campus—somebody's going to have to get appraisal planning organized to placate Mid-Central—and, at the same time, to gain some experience with administration that might, in turn, lead to bigger things. Besides, he won't have to teach as many classes, and everyone will sympathize that his new job makes it impossible to pursue research (so he won't face pressure to publish). Thirdtier begins to pay Professor Bertram's way to conferences where people from various colleges meet to discuss the nature of appraisal planning, methods of implementation, and so on. In addition to providing information he can bring back to Thirdtier, these conferences offer Prof. Bertram chances to meet administrators at other colleges, and you never know when those contacts might come in handy.

Like Professor Alice, Professor Bertram finds that an institutional fad—in this case, appraisal planning—opens career opportunities. In addition to doing good (by leading Thirdtier's efforts to catch up to what at least some people say is an important trend in higher education), Professor Bertram will be doing well (in a job that seems better suited to his talents, pays more, and offers the prospect of other, even better jobs). There are clear advantages to riding the appraisal planning wave, and no serious risks. Dean Daniel and Provost Elaine anticipate parallel advantages. Both have ambitions for larger things—Dean Daniel wouldn't mind being a provost, and Provost Elaine likes to think she'd make a fine college president—but they need to demonstrate that they have the right stuff to move up. Supervising the implementation of Thirdtier's appraisal plan, and earning a favorable accreditation review from Mid-Central, might be a good way to highlight their administrative talents.

Professor Alice, Professor Bertram, Dean Daniel, and Provost Elaine all find good reasons to buy into the institutional fads of chaos theory or appraisal planning. They illustrate the importance of *careerism*—making choices that will advance one's career—in the spread of such fads. People who work within institutions have to worry about their personal careers. Individuals will have various personal goals: some want security; others seek new challenges; and most want to make a good impression on other people, whether those people are customers, clients, colleagues, bosses, or stockholders. Whether they are scheming to rocket to the top or just hoping to hang on to the jobs they have, individuals need to give some thought to their careers.

And novelties can give careers a boost.[20] Whenever an organization adopts an innovation, there is the possibility that parts of

---

OFFICE FOLKLORE ON THE IMPACT
OF REORGANIZATION

We trained hard—but it seemed that every time we were beginning to form up into teams we would be reorganized. . . . I was to
learn later in life that we tend to meet any new situation by re-
organizing; and a wonderful method it can be for creating the illusion of progress while producing confusion, inefficiency, and
demoralization.

—Petronius Arbiter, 210 B.C.E. [Note: this attribution is incorrect (as is Petronius's
date; he died ca. 66 C.E.). Versions of this bit of office folklore have been in circulation since at least the 1970s.]

Source: Dundes and Pagter (2000: 20).

---

that organization will change. Maybe new jobs, such as director of
appraisal planning, will appear (and perhaps some old jobs will disappear); maybe the organization will begin doing different things,
or at least start doing some things differently. The organization will
be—at least to some degree—in flux, which will almost certainly
create opportunities. How individuals respond to those opportunities may affect their careers. Remember that novelties are billed as
the route to progress. Individuals who—and organizations that—
are receptive to change are seen as adaptable, flexible, and welcoming the future rather than mired in the past, unable to "think
outside the box" of tradition. And, of course, if a novelty comes
endorsed by your supervisors—if, say, campus leaders have
decreed their commitment to appraisal planning, or company executives have heralded a new management philosophy—actively
resisting the change may put your career at risk. It can be much
easier to go along with the changes (see box above).

Careerist considerations affect even those near the top of their
organizations' ladders. Presidents and CEOs worry about the

dangers of complacency and standing pat. Rival firms are plotting to increase their market share, to get ahead at our expense. Therefore, organizational leaders need to pay attention and spot promising trends. The news that someone, somewhere has gotten good results from some innovation suggests that maybe our organization ought to follow their lead. (Recognize that in any large institution, it is probably always true that somebody out there is getting relatively good results doing something, making it possible to spot prospective leaders who might be followed on the basis of their recent successes.)[21] It can't hurt to try the novelty. And what if we don't adopt this new approach and our rivals do; what if this innovation really works, and we let our rivals take advantage of it, and they get the jump on us? Even on the top rungs of the organizational ladder, adopting institutional fads can boost careers, or at least help you ward off criticism that you aren't keeping up to date.

Of course, calculated decisions to adopt a novelty usually depend on the assumption that others will continue to support this trend. Just as speculators join a bull market assuming that other investors will continue buying and thereby raise prices further, so too the adoption of institutional fads is attractive because of not just what others have done but what they are expected to continue doing. Given this assumption, adoption minimizes the risk that you might be wrong while your competitors are right.[22] This reasoning seems compelling to many—but not to all.

LAGGARDS AND RESISTERS

In spite of the emotional satisfactions and calculated advantages of adopting innovations, some people are slow to go along with the crowd. Social scientific studies of diffusion sometimes refer to these late adopters as *laggards*.[23] This rather pejorative label reveals diffusion researchers' underlying assumption that innovation is part of the march of progress. The classic studies of diffusion focused on what were seen as unambiguously positive innovations (the spread of hybrid seed corn among Iowa farmers, the willingness of Illinois doctors to prescribe an improved antibiotic, and so on), so researchers tended to see reluctance to adopt as a problem that needed to be explained.

Not surprisingly, then, researchers are apt to portray late adopters in rather negative terms. For instance, in his classic analysis of diffusion, Everett Rogers gives the following description of laggards:

> Many are near isolates in the social networks of their system. . . . [T]hese individuals interact primarily with others who also have relatively traditional values. Laggards tend to be suspicious of innovations. . . . Their innovation-decision process is lengthy, with adoption and use lagging far behind awareness-knowledge of a new idea. . . . Their resources are limited and they must be certain that a new idea will not fail before they can adopt.[24]

However well this portrait may fit people who are slow to join the process of diffusion, we might wonder whether it is equally appropriate when the innovations in question are less lasting. Few people, once they had telephones or television sets, chose to give them up. But fads are transitory; most individuals—or, in the case of institutional fads, most organizations—that adopt the novelty later (and usually not all that much later) abandon it. This means that even as laggards are joining some fad, at least some of the early adopters who set the trend may have already dropped it. Thus, the laggards are out of sync, perpetually behind the cutting edge. By adopting styles or fashions late, after they have already begun to lose favor among the cognoscenti, laggards only marginalize themselves further. Refusing to adopt the novelty when it first spreads, then finally taking it up after the trendsetters have begun to abandon it, makes these laggards always seem dated, out of step, not with it.

But why adopt an innovation that is already losing its popularity? The obvious answer is that laggards don't realize that the fad is fading. They don't get the word, in part because laggards are less well connected to social networks, less aware of what's going on, less conscious of current developments and what the trendsetters are doing today.

In the case of institutional fads, there are other reasons laggards may find it hard to follow current trends. The media tend to celebrate innovation on its arrival, as when the business press reports that hundreds of major corporations are adopting some new management approach. But there is far less coverage when the novelty begins to be dropped. A corporation may issue a press release trumpeting that it has adopted the new management technique, but it is unlikely to publicize its later decision to abandon the scheme. After all, why draw attention to your false starts or failures?

Note, too, that an organization may not make a clear decision to drop the fad; fads often fade away quietly and gradually. The original schedule for implementing the new program in all of the organization's units may be extended or postponed; the money budgeted to support the innovation may be—temporarily, of course—less than originally promised; it may gradually become apparent that the firm's key leaders don't seem to be basing their decisions on the information generated in the required reports—all of these are little clues that the fad is falling out of favor. Abandoning a fad is often a subtle, silent process. Even if other corporations are doing the same thing and quietly abandoning the innovation, when none of them broadcasts the news of their retreat then each company may assume that its failure is atypical, that its competitors are having more success with the innovation—so why proclaim your own disappointment? The media, too, have their own reasons for keeping quiet: why announce the failure of an innovation that you earlier heralded for its transformative power when, instead, you can cover a more appealing story—the emergence of the next novelty?[25]

As a result, those laggards who are a little out of the loop may be forgiven for still believing that an innovation represents diffusion—that is, real, enduring change, something that everybody else is still doing—even after the innovation's actual popularity is declining among the early adopters. In fact, some research suggests that both individuals and organizations that are late adopters base their decisions less on the supposed merits of the novelty than on their desire to follow in the footsteps of others they admire.[26] Failure to grasp that a fad is already losing favor is particularly likely when novelties spread across institutional boundaries. For example, higher education administrators tend to copy management fads that begin in business or government. However, because colleges and universities aren't especially well-connected to business and government networks, they are continually laggards. Because they learn about new management techniques late and are slower to adopt them, management innovations often enter the world of higher education after they have already begun being abandoned in the institutions where they emerged.[27]

Portraying laggards as rather hapless figures—out of touch, suspicious of change, unimaginative, reluctant to spend money on new things—gives them little credit, and ignores how some people who are reluctant to adopt an innovation may see their actions in positive terms. Consider the attractions of a knowing, cynical stance. Refusing to go along with the enthusiasm for an innovation may give at least some people a sense of satisfaction and status. It is possible to affect a worldly, cynical, I've-seen-'em-come-and-I've-seen-'em-go attitude toward proposed changes. While sometimes a lone individual may make an iconoclastic stand, such independence often isn't necessary when there is a loose network of support for skeptical resistance.[28] In particular, resistance can be made appealing by grounding it in humor rather than anger. Making fun of the foibles of those who rush to adopt the newest novelty can attract supporters.

This cynical stance is revealed in the huge body of *photocopier folklore*—the various subversively comic cartoons, slogans, and bogus memos that one sees posted in offices (for examples, see "The Six Stages of a Project" discussed in chapter 1, or the boxed material on p. 101 and elsewhere in this chapter).[29] Technology has given a tremendous boost to these expressions of disenchantment—photocopiers, then fax machines, e-mail, improved printers, and most recently the ability to attach drawings, photos, and other graphics to e-mail messages have made it much easier for people to duplicate and circulate these materials. The means of reproduction, at least, are in the hands of the people. In addition, humorous expressions of organizational alienation have been turned into successful commercial ventures; consider the popu-

EXPRESSIONS OF DISENCHANTMENT
Educators' Folklore

Horse Story

Common advice from knowledgeable horse trainers includes the adage, "If the horse you're riding dies, get off." Seems simple enough, yet, in the education business we don't always follow that advice. Instead, we often choose from an array of alternatives which include:

1. Buying a stronger whip.
2. Trying a new bit or bridle.
3. Switching riders.
4. Moving the horse to a new location.
5. Riding the horse for longer periods of time.
6. Saying things like, "This is the way we've always ridden this horse."
7. Appointing a committee to study the horse.
8. Arranging to visit other sites where they ride dead horses efficiently.
9. Increasing the standards for riding dead horses.
10. Creating a test for measuring our riding ability.
11. Comparing how we're riding now with how we did 10 or 20 years ago.
12. Complaining about the state of horses these days.
13. Coming up with new styles of riding.
14. Blaming the horse's parents. The problem is often in the breeding.
15. Tightening the cinch.

—In circulation in the early 1990s

Source: Sarason (1996: 315).

larity of the *Dilbert* comic strip or the "demotivating" posters sold by Despair.com.[30]

One attraction of such humor is that it is ambiguous. Is the cynic a serious critic, or is this really just a joke? The uncertainty means that it is possible to stick some amusing expression of subversive sentiment above your desk without actually refusing to comply with your organization's policies, and anyone who criticizes your joke risks being accused of lacking a sense of humor.

There are other ways to refuse to get with the program, to resist change within your organization. It is easy for management to announce that an organization will implement some new program. It is much more difficult to get everyone to comply, particularly if they suspect they have something to lose by the change. Resistance can take many forms: the required reports may not arrive on time, or the information they contain may be inaccurate, or—any canny subordinate in a large organization knows that there are countless ways to work the system to an underling's own advantage. While it may take time to figure out how to adapt to the new management scheme, people can usually find ways around the constraints posed by innovations.

When an innovation threatens established interests, resistance can become organized. For example, some recent efforts to use standardized testing to make schools more accountable have confronted active opposition from teachers' unions. Recall that successful novelties often appeal to people with a broad range of views; it is difficult to force change upon organized opponents.

Finally, we should recognize that some people—and some organizations—may consider, and then refuse to adopt, innovations for more or less principled reasons. Thus, parents often hold strong beliefs about the appropriateness of spanking: some believe that spanking is necessary, while others view it as unacceptable. The announcement that the newest child-development guru has written a best seller that endorses—or denounces—spanking is not likely to sway parents who are deeply attached to the opposing view. Rather, they are likely to dismiss the new book and think, "That's not how I want to raise my child." Similarly, organizations have their own cultures, their own understandings about the kind of things they do. If an organization's members see a new management fad as somehow inconsistent with their culture, they are unlikely to adopt that innovation.[31] When people can articulate what they see as good reasons not to adopt a novelty, they probably won't become adopters.

Here, we should not overlook what sociologists call *inertia*.[32] Organizations and institutions become invested in particular social arrangements. For example, symphony orchestras have evolved to contain musicians trained to play certain instruments, using a standard system of musical notation, and so on. These arrangements become taken for granted; we tend to forget that there are lots of alternative ways of making music, using all sorts of other instruments, other systems of notation, and such. It is relatively easy for an orchestra to expand its repertoire—so long as we compose a piece for the usual instruments, using standard notation sheet music. But it would be terribly difficult for musicians to learn to play unfamiliar instruments, using a score based on an unorthodox notation system. Such an undertaking would require a huge investment in new instruments, time to learn to play them and to master the alternative system of notation, and so on. The cost is probably too high, and the risk—Would audiences come to hear a completely different form of music?—too great. Inertia encourages symphonies to stick fairly close to what they already know how to do rather than venturing far afield.

Obviously, all institutions have their own cultures and structures within which they are used to operating—they all face analogous forms of inertia. Promoters are fond of breakthrough rhetoric, of announcing paradigm shifts and revolutionary changes. They declare that they will "reinvent government," "revolutionize education," and "transform medicine." They hype their novelties as something completely different. But, for the most part, their innovations tend to be relatively modest and respect institutional inertia far more than they require fundamental changes. Just as it is relatively easy to, say, write, rehearse, and play symphony arrangements of pop songs but impractical to change all the instruments, the musical notation system, and the type of pieces performed for each concert, so institutional fads tend to present innovations that don't change things too much. To propose more radical changes is to invite resistance.

BEYOND INEVITABILITY

The excitement experienced by those involved with a surging innovation encourages people to view the change as inevitable. Each new adopter seems to confirm that *this* is the direction in which the world is changing—surging is the stage when the illusion of diffusion is most widespread. It is important to remember that for each successful innovation—whether it is a new diet or a new management scheme—there are many, many competing novelties that have failed to make the grade. Each of these new offerings was launched with high hopes. Doubtless their odds of success varied. We can presume that innovations promoted by already visible figures have brighter prospects than those offered by unknowns. No doubt a big budget or a savvy public relations campaign can help get a novelty off the ground. But, ultimately, success depends on countless decisions by individuals and organizations to adopt something new. Even in the most sophisticated fashion industries, outcomes are uncertain: movie studios can't be sure how many people will go to see next week's release, and high-fashion designers can't know which dress designs will capture the fashion world's imagination.

The same uncertainty holds for institutional fads. The excitements of being part of a surge, as well as calculations that this innovation can boost one's career or the profits of one's firm, lead people to become adopters. But success is anything but inevitable—and in the case of fads, neither is it permanent.

5

The Fad Cycle

Purging

───────────

Around 1990, public attention became focused on the prospect that bone marrow transplants might cure women with advanced breast cancer. Physicians had tried the procedure a few times, and some of the results seemed promising. While research was still in its early stages, the media began publicizing the potential break-through, and patients started approaching doctors to request that they be given the treatment, which they saw as their only hope. However, bone marrow transplants involved several weeks of hospitalization, with total costs often exceeding $100,000, and some medical insurers refused to cover the costs of a treatment that had not been proven effective. This became a public issue, with numerous newspaper editorials and talk show episodes devoted to the topic. The story lent itself to melodramatic coverage, in which mothers of loving families who were threatened by a fatal disease could be cured by heroic doctors armed with a miraculous new treatment, if only grasping insurance companies would not refuse to pay for the potentially lifesaving treatment. Not surprisingly, public opinion stood with the patients rather than the insurers. Legislators began insisting that insurance companies cover the costs of the transplants: let the patients have the treatment that might save their lives.

Just a few years later, the enthusiasm for bone marrow transplants as a treatment for advanced breast cancer had faded. More patients had been treated using the procedure, their progress had been systematically compared to that of patients receiving other treatments, and the results of these experiments showed that receiving bone marrow transplants did not extend patients' lives any more than the standard treatments. That is, the new treatment was not more effective than existing treatments, although it cost considerably more. The calls to make bone marrow transplants available to patients with advanced breast cancer ended.[1]

There is nothing very surprising about this story. This is, after all, how medical science is supposed to advance: researchers develop a hypothesis that some treatment ought to work, they conduct experimental research in which patients receiving the new treatment are compared to a control group (which usually receives the best alternative treatment), and the results are assessed. If the new treatment turns out to be more effective in treating the disease, this news spreads throughout the medical establishment, and other doctors adopt the innovation. But if the new treatment cannot be shown to be somehow superior, it is set aside and eventually abandoned. Such failures are disappointing, but they are clear-cut, given the assumptions of rationality and progress that underpin scientific medicine.

It is tempting to assume that this is somehow the fate of all institutional fads, that they fade—and fads do, by definition, fade—after they are shown to be ineffective.[2] Institutional fads are promoted as solutions to problems; presumably, a fad will be rejected when—and because—it is apparent that this solution doesn't work.

Unfortunately, the actual process by which fads are abandoned—what I am calling *purging*—is rather more complicated. Tests of effectiveness turn out to be less important than we might imagine; ineffective innovations aren't necessarily abandoned. Moreover, just as institutional fads emerge and surge on the basis of weak evidence for a novelty's value, so purging often occurs before there is strong proof of its ineffectiveness. Ultimately, to understand why fads fade, we need to consider other explanations.

FAILURE'S AMBIGUOUS IMPACT

Consider DARE—the Drug Abuse Resistance Education program. Launched around the time that the war on drugs took off in the mid-1980s, DARE quickly became the leading drug prevention program aimed at schoolchildren; in recent years, a substantial majority of American school districts offered DARE training. Typically, schools present DARE as a one-week unit during fourth or fifth grade. The children are taught something about the dangers of drugs, but much of the program focuses on videos, role-playing, and other lessons designed to teach children ways they can refuse when invited to use drugs. DARE is presented in cooperation with local police departments; an officer makes presentations to the classes. At the end of the unit, there is a graduation ceremony, and children are given red ribbons, T-shirts, or other trinkets featuring the DARE logo.

Like many programs that are widely adopted, DARE appeals to a broad range of ideological views. Liberals, who often complain that the drug war places too much emphasis on punishment and too little on prevention and treatment, are favorably disposed toward drug-prevention programs such as DARE. Conservatives, who in the early years of the war on drugs promoted First Lady Nancy Reagan's slogan, "Just Say No," approve of a program that centers on teaching children how to say no (and that has the cooperation and endorsement of local police). Offering DARE lets schools claim that they are doing their part to inoculate children against drug use. There's really only one small problem.

There is a good deal of evidence indicating that DARE doesn't work.[3] Well-designed experiments that follow children who have completed DARE training and compare their level of drug use to that among a control group that hasn't gone through the program fail to show that DARE has a significant effect. (Obviously, good experiments need to match the students exposed to DARE and the control group as closely as possible in terms of potentially relevant variables, such as social class, academic achievement, etc.) To be sure, there are students who pass through DARE who go on to never use drugs—but this turns out to be about equally true for students who are not exposed to DARE; similarly, the proportions who go on to use drugs are about equal in the DARE groups and the control groups. In short, research suggests that DARE is no more effective at preventing drug use than bone marrow transplants were in controlling advanced breast cancer; in both cases, experimental research failed to find that either program worked better than existing alternatives.

The difference is that DARE has survived. Its proponents insist that it does work. They offer anecdotal proof; according to one local official: "If [skeptics] could just see the kids' faces they'd know how much good it's doing."[4] Besides, everyone agrees that drug prevention is desirable; if we don't use DARE, what program will we offer? DARE's defenders also insist that their program is evolving, improving. Most studies of DARE measure drug use during junior high or high school (that is, a few years after the students took DARE training), and it probably takes at least a couple of years for researchers to collect their data, conduct the analysis, and publish their results. This means that most published studies evaluate the effectiveness of the DARE training given at least four or five years earlier. It is always possible to argue that however flawed the old program may have been, today's new, improved DARE is far more effective. Of course, it will take more years to test that claim, at which point, even if those results are disappointing, its defenders should be able to insist that DARE has evolved still further.

In other words, rather than fading away, DARE continues in spite of the lack of strong evidence supporting the program's effectiveness. The contrast with the fate of bone marrow transplant therapy for advanced breast cancer is striking: the absence of supporting evidence ended the enthusiasm for the medical treatment, but it seems to have had little effect on the drug-prevention program. Note that in both cases, the evidence in question came from relatively well-designed experiments that compared those exposed to the innovation with control groups. In other words, the question was not whether some patient who received a bone marrow transplant experienced improvements, or whether some DARE graduates stay drug-free, but whether either innovation was more likely to work than whatever else might be done. In both cases, the answer was that the program being tested was not more effective than the alternatives.

So how can we explain DARE's survival, and the abandonment

of bone marrow transplants for treating breast cancer? First, it should be obvious that the culture of science values experimental evidence. New scientific ideas need to be tested, ideally using experimental designs, and ideas that can't survive such tests are supposed to be dropped.[5] To be sure, science does not have an unblemished record in this regard; critics like to point to embarrassing episodes in its history—scientific ideas that suffered rejection, only to be revived later; scientists who cling to their hypotheses long after most other scientists have abandoned them; or scientists who fudge their results.[6] Still, in general and over the long haul, scientists recognize that their disciplines advance through a process of rejecting ideas that cannot find empirical support, and proponents of scientific medicine endorse this principle. Thus, any new medical treatment can expect to be subjected to testing that could lead to its being rejected.

In contrast, other institutions, such as education, business, and criminal justice, have weaker commitments to the values of science, and place less emphasis on research-based evidence.[7] For one thing, such research often takes a long time and costs lots of money, so the studies tend to follow, rather than precede, the adoption of innovations. I have already suggested that institutional fads emerge and surge on the basis of weak evidence, generally anecdotal reports of successes and the news that others have adopted the novelty. Academic researchers aren't always quick to pick up on the new trends, and it takes additional time for them to design their research, acquire the necessary funding and permissions, gather their data, complete their analyses, and publish the results. By the time the research process is completed, many fads already have begun to fade—and indeed have virtually vanished.[8]

The example of DARE is a reminder that innovations have

SKEPTICISM ABOUT CLAIMS OF
A PROGRAM'S EFFECTIVENESS

The professor addressed the class: "Seated around a table in a restaurant were a high-priced lawyer, the CEO of a company performing at true Six Sigma, Snow White, and Santa Claus. The door opened and a cloaked visitor walked in, and on their table dropped $250,000 in cash, right in the middle of the table. Instantly the lights went out. A moment later, the lights came back on, and the money had disappeared. Who had the money!?!?"

A moment later, a reply came from the best student in the class: "The high-priced lawyer had the money."

"That is correct. And why the high-priced lawyer?"

"Because the other three were figments of our imagination."

— Joke circulating on the Internet

---

defenders, and that evidence-based challenges will not necessarily end their spread. All sorts of arguments to defend novelties in the face of disconfirming evidence are possible. For instance, if studies show that a management scheme works only in a minority of cases, the program's promoters might still praise those managers who are bold enough to risk likely failure in the hope of becoming one of the successes.[9] In short, it is usually possible to put a positive spin on bad news. Thus, the explanation that somehow evidence accounts for the demise of institutional fads is far too simplistic (see box above).

WHY SOME CHANGES ENDURE

The time required to conduct evaluation studies doesn't fully explain DARE's resilience. Even if it takes years to test the program's effectiveness, shouldn't the negative results have damaged the program? The question ignores the importance of *institutionalization*—the process by which promoters establish enduring arrangements to support new developments. Consider the notion of hate crimes. Activists in the early 1980s began arguing that crimes motivated by racial or religious bias were different—and needed to be treated as more serious—than crimes involving greed, jealousy, or other more mundane motives. Over time, the concept evolved: the term *hate crime* replaced *bias crime;* the categories of victims expanded, particularly to include gays and lesbians; states and the federal government began passing laws defining hate crimes and establishing punishments for these offenses; the media began carrying hate-crime stories; funds became available to support research on hate crimes; and so on. Hate crimes, in short, became a well-established, institutionalized part of the American criminal justice landscape—a case of legal diffusion, rather than just a passing fad.[10]

Institutionalization is important, because it establishes an enduring niche for an innovation, making it much harder to dislodge. We can think of diffusion—the enduring spread of some novelty—as taking two forms. One form involves the choices of many individuals who discover the value of some innovation, such as wristwatches or cell phones. People are free to choose to adopt the novelty, and they are free to abandon it—but they don't give it up, because it somehow serves their needs: it is convenient to wear a watch or carry a phone.

The other form of diffusion involves the establishment of institutional arrangements that make it harder to drop the innovation. Thus, once there are hate-crime laws, court decisions affirming the legitimacy of those laws, police trained to enforce the laws, funding agencies supporting research on hate crimes, and so on, these social arrangements establish a lasting place for the new crime. DARE is a good example of such institutionalization. Thousands of schools have established drug-prevention partnerships with local police departments. Millions of dollars are being spent on DARE-based educational materials. As a consequence, evidence questioning the program's effectiveness confronts not just proponents' insistence that what they're doing should work, and therefore must be working, but also the inertia of large organizations that have trouble identifying an alternate course of action—it is easier to keep on presenting DARE programs.[11]

Innovations are more likely to become institutionalized when they inspire little overt opposition. After all, there are few voices speaking in favor of hate crimes or against drug prevention. It also helps if there is broad, enthusiastic support for the novelty. Ideally, such support will come from both within and outside the affected institution (thus, DARE tends to be viewed positively not just by educators and police, but also by the local press and parents), and also from different levels within the institution (so that DARE needs the support of classroom teachers, as well as school principals and district superintendents). Such support is easier to come by if the innovation does not disrupt existing arrangements within the institution (for instance, because DARE offers a package of lesson plans and other instructional aids and can be offered as a one-week unit, the program minimizes both the amount of extra work required from teachers and the disruption in their schedules). Also, innovations that spread more gradually, so that they have more time to establish their base of supporters, are more likely to endure than novelties that spread like wildfire. In other words, under certain conditions innovations are more likely to become institutionalized or entrenched.[12] Where those conditions do not hold, novelties are more likely to peak and fade.

PEAKING: THE BEGINNING OF THE END

If contrary evidence has little effect, then how should we explain the purging of institutional fads? Many analysts argue that in order for institutional fads to surge, to achieve the success of widespread adoption, their character must evolve. Remember that later adopters are more likely to be interested in and motivated by knowing that many others have adopted an innovation than they are to be attracted by the novelty's putative merits. That is, as an innovation spreads, the later adopters are less likely to focus on how well the novelty works, or even to understand its principles all that well. In fact, in order to reach more adopters, promoters may dilute the content of their presentations to make the innovation seem easier to grasp and thus more broadly appealing.[13] To the degree that those who stand to benefit more from a novelty are more likely to adopt earlier in its spread, later adopters may have less to gain from the innovation.[14] At the same time, having heard lots of success stories about others' experiences, later adopters may have more exaggerated and unrealistic expectations for what adoption will bring.[15] Thus, many of these people are primed for disappointment.

Meanwhile, those who were quicker to adopt also are becoming restive. Whatever cachet there may have been in early adoption has diminished as the bandwagon has become more crowded. As Joseph Epstein observes, "Without a feeling of exclusiveness—the snobbish element—fashion isn't successfully fashion-able."[16] The once-trendy innovation has become passé, unfash-ionable; in fact, this process can accelerate as people start mut-tering the F-words, dismissing the novelty as just a fad or a passing fashion.[17] Decreasing trendiness is reflected in a drop in media coverage. The media want to cover what's new; that some now-familiar innovation has continued to spread increasingly looks like old news, not really worth mentioning.[18]

Also, to the degree that early adopters were prestigious figures, whom others might want to copy for their daring, imag-ination, and cutting-edge reputations, the later adopters seem more ordinary. While early adopters may have benefited from an appealing snob effect, the spectacle of late adopters clambering aboard conveys a "mob effect."[19] This is an example of a more general process of *symbolic inflation*—that is, as any social symbol becomes more widespread (for example, if more and more schools adopt some educational reform), the value of that symbol falls (later adopters receive relatively less credit for being inno-vative when they finally do come around).[20] Whatever advantages there may have been to being one of the few associated with a hot new novelty decline as the number of adopters swells, and the bandwagon becomes crowded.[21] Thus, the rewards for being an adopter shrink as the innovation spreads.

This means that for individuals, the major careerist advan-tages come from adopting the innovation rather than from stick-ing with it. "Fashions 'wear out through use'"; that is, any inno-vation becomes familiar, and therefore less interesting, even as its limitations become more apparent.[22] Whatever advantage might come from being associated with the glistening, idealistic expec-tations for a newly adopted novelty is reduced by real-world experience with a tarnished reality that doesn't live up to the innovation's advance billing. In particular, there may be very little benefit in waiting for research evidence that assesses the novelty's value: "The career pay-off may simply be in being seen as innovative.... Given the short time focus of the managerial world, managers are encouraged to move away from the last 'assignment' and on to the next without risking systematic evaluation and the attendant possibility of criticism."[23] Far better for one's career to simply declare victory, to announce that the innovation made an important contribution (in which you were involved), and to move on to embrace the next novelty.[24]

In other words, institutional fads approach a tipping point.[25] As the peak approaches, those who have adopted the innovation find that they have fewer, weaker reasons to continue their involvement. If the novelty has become institutionalized, along the lines of DARE or hate-crime legislation, it is harder to abandon it. But institutional fads tend to have few of the trappings of institutionalization.[26] Oh, there may be a special job title here and there (remember Thirdtier College's director of appraisal planning) that will need to be changed (and its occupant reassigned to other duties), but most people and organizations are not so heavily invested that they can't abandon the fad. The end begins to prey on their minds. John Kenneth Galbraith describes investors in financial bubbles as "programmed for sudden efforts at escape.... [T]he speculative episode always ends not with a whimper but with a bang."[27]

The collapse of institutional fads tends to be less sudden. Even before the fad peaks, the trendsetters may already have begun leaving. If the fad has spread across institutional boundaries, it may begin its decline in the originating institution, even as it

---

NOT EVERYONE GETS THE WORD
AT THE SAME TIME

A few years ago I read about administrators at a middle school in San Diego, where I now live, who wanted a fresh teaching plan for their new charter school and chose the team-teaching model. Meanwhile, a few miles away, another middle school was in the process of abandoning that same model because it hadn't had any effect on the students' grades.

—Essay by a former teacher
Source: Keliher (2002: 18).

---

continues to spread in institutions where it caught on later (thus, administrators in both schools and colleges often adopt management fads after businesses have begun to reject them).[28] Researchers who study the fad's impact—because they need lots of time to become aware of the novelty, identify it as a potential subject for study, carry out their research, and then make the results known—almost invariably lag behind the trend; their studies' findings, pro or con, thus appear after many adopters have already lost interest.[29] As a result, the collapse of institutional fads is not nearly as sudden or panicky as speculators fleeing a bear market (see box above).

Of course, at bottom, institutional fads begin to fade because they haven't fulfilled their promise. The new management scheme hasn't suddenly turned the firms that adopted it into industry leaders. The new medical treatment isn't miraculously curing all the patients who receive it. The new reading program hasn't transformed all students into above-grade-level readers. Having been promoted as dramatic breakthroughs, and having failed to live up to those expectations, institutional fads begin to slip.

THE PROCESS OF DECLINE

Here, it may help to consider this chapter's imaginary figure—Wiley, a middle manager in a large corporation. A couple of years ago, he attended the firm's annual meeting, where it was announced that the corporation was adopting the Acme Bottom-Line Management program (ABLM). Acme—a leading management consulting firm—was promoting ABLM as a revolutionary management system. In their presentations, the consultants explained that too many managers tended to get fixated on unimportant details, and failed to remain focused on the bottom line. This insight didn't strike Wiley as all that blinding, but ABLM offered sets of guidelines, rules, principles, and slogans (e.g., "Getting to the Top Requires Keeping an Eye on the Bottom [Line]") that promised a fresh approach to corporate success. Later, Wiley was sent to workshops: first, ABLM Basic Training, then an ABLM Masters' Session (where Wiley received a diploma that certified him as having become an "ABLMaster"). Following his training, he was charged with handling the ABLM evaluations and planning for his division.

Wiley has begun having mixed feelings about ABLM. On the one hand, attending those training sessions was a good career move: once he became an ABLMaster, he received a new assignment, with a special title and a modestly higher salary, which involved preparing special ABLM analyses that were supposed to go directly to his division's leaders. But otherwise, things haven't changed all that much. The corporation's profits haven't jumped, and Wiley's division has had trouble meeting many of its ABLM goals. His ABLM-based recommendations seem to have less and less influence on his division leadership's decision making, and

Wiley no longer has the sense that he's in line for another quick promotion up the corporate ladder. Wiley doesn't think that ABLM has made all that much difference to the corporation's operations, and he gets the sense that neither the people he reports to nor the people who report to him have all that much faith in the power of ABLM. These are all signs that ABLM is on its way out.

Institutional fads lose support because people like Wiley redefine the novelty's meaning. What was formerly viewed as a breakthrough comes to be seen as a disappointment, even a failure. Problems become apparent: "the package becomes rigidified, costs exceed benefits, the novelty wears off, and substitutes appear on the scene."[30] The process may be gradual and occur without ever being acknowledged. For instance, a study of schools that had abandoned fluoride mouth rinse programs found that in most cases, there was no "formal decision process" that led to halting the program.[31]

Analysts use various terms to characterize the process of decline, such as *deinstitutionalization, rollback,* or *fade-out.*[32] Whatever it is called, the process involves people abandoning the hopes that led them to adopt the fad as the solution to their problems. Even gurus may begin backpedaling, qualifying their promises.[33] The innovation no longer seems to embody progress.[34] Growing doubts may make people less willing to spend money and other resources on the novelty, and tighter resources in turn make success less likely.[35] Rather, people now focus on their disappointment, on the gap between the solution that the fad promised and whatever the novelty actually delivered. They may have been enthusiastic when they adopted the fad, but now their criticisms are dispassionate and carefully reasoned. Adopters become openly skeptical about the innovation's value, while the resisters who never did get behind the program sense that the momentum has turned.[36] These skeptics may organize in opposition to the fad, developing what some call *counterfashions* or *counterbandwagons.*[37] What triggers the decline? Analysts distinguish between *collapse triggers,* or growing disenchantment with an already adopted innovation, and *elimination triggers,* or growing interest in some alternative novelty that might replace the one losing favor. Collapse triggers occur in all institutional fads; elimination triggers may accompany them, but aren't necessary. When adopters drop a fad because they are dissatisfied with its performance (that is, when there are collapse triggers), they are said to be *debunking.* However, when elimination triggers invite the managers to "slide smoothly from one strategy to the next," those adopters are said to be *surfing*—as in catching the next wave.[38]

Surfing from one innovation to the next is particularly common in the case of management fads: alternatives are readily available because promoters and their publishers and consulting firms are conscious of the huge, ongoing demand for fresh management schemes, understand how to go about promoting novelties, and, knowing the track record of earlier fads that have died out, anticipate that new opportunities will arise. "The process of management fad displacement" is not difficult: "the so-called 'new' solutions offered . . . tend to be similar to those which preceded them. Thus, 'old' products can be easily displaced with little psychological pain to managers, because the new ones are so similar."[39] It is not hard to mount a new campaign: "a brain, a personal computer, and a web page are becoming the only entry barriers."[40] But if you do succeed in replacing an earlier fad, you shouldn't forget that it will be equally easy for the next innovation to arrive and replace yours, as yet another new wave attracts those disenchanted surfers.

To be sure, everyone doesn't abandon a fad simultaneously. Some people are slower to recognize collapse triggers: one study found that physicians who didn't keep up with the professional literature were more likely to continue prescribing a drug after research reports questioned its value.[41] Similarly, people become aware of new innovations—that is, elimination triggers—at different times. And just as there are late adopters who are slow to climb on the bandwagon, so any fad may develop loyalists reluctant to abandon their favorite innovation. They may complain that what others are purging as a fad wasn't given a fair shake. The innovation could have, should have worked, they insist, but it wasn't given a decent shot. There were too many naysayers, and they were allowed to sabotage the project. The organization's leadership didn't commit themselves to the innovation's success. The budget wasn't sufficient, implementation wasn't thorough and complete, and the new program wasn't given enough time to show what it could accomplish. In these loyalists' view, abandoning the fad says more about the weak character of fickle adopters than it does about the innovation's merits.[42]

Besides, the rejection need not be total. Even an abandoned fad may leave a residue or sediments.[43] Some elements are abandoned more slowly. Perhaps these are things seen as having greater value, as those elements of the innovation deemed most useful and therefore worth retaining. Or perhaps they are elements that have somehow become more entrenched or better institutionalized; for example, people now have standard procedures for gathering particular information for inclusion in their reports. And just as some adopters are late to get on board a new fad, there are those who are slower to abandon what others have already rejected.

There is some evidence that at least among fads in management and education, the emerging–surging–purging sequence is becoming more extreme.[44] That is, the time between a fad's introduction and its abandonment is growing shorter, yet each successive fad seems to generate more enthusiasm—more media coverage and the like. The peaks are growing higher and sharper. The question is, what should we make of this?

AFTERMATH

This chapter and the previous two have examined the life cycle of institutional fads: emerging amid promises of solutions to serious problems, surging as people and organizations scramble aboard the bandwagon, and then purging as the fad peaks and adopters begin distancing themselves from their former enthusiasm.

How should we view this process? It is easy to see its comic qualities, as serious people latch onto ideas that they will later reject as silly, as they insist that all the evidence favors adopting the novelty (while ignoring just how skimpy and flimsy that evidence is), as they assume a mantle of prescience that they will soon shed. Similarly, it is easy to think of some fads' promoters as amusing figures. Our culture has a history of enjoying the antics of hucksters and flimflam artists—P. T. Barnum, the Duke of Bilgewater, and on and on. Talk of management witchdoctors and gurus—terms used by their followers as well as their critics—has at least overtones of irony. In retrospect, for those who adopt a comic stance, all fads, from hula hoops to Total Quality Management, seem inexplicable—just funny, weird episodes in the march of progress (see box on page 125).

However, not everyone is laughing. Institutional fads can be seen as serious matters by both their defenders and their critics. The defenders may acknowledge that a particular fad proved disappointing, worthless, even harmful, yet they find value in the cycle of institutional fads. These defenders can be divided into those who view institutional fads as rational and those who emphasize the fads' emotional benefits.

The defenders who stress rationality tend to have backgrounds in economics or organizational studies—disciplines that seek to account for people's behavior as the product of rational choices. In their view, an organization's managers are—and should be—rational decision makers. If they choose to adopt some new management approach, that choice must be a reaction to the organization's environment (that is, their decision reflects how managers assess the entire array of customers, competitors, employees, and other folks who come into contact with their firm), as well as their sense of the challenges and opportunities they confront. Thus, a choice to adopt a new management scheme should be seen as a product of rational calculations; and if, not too much later, the same managers choose to switch to yet another management approach, that decision, too, must reflect a rational assessment of a changing situation. Perhaps the rejected scheme failed to live up to expectations, but then again, perhaps it was successful—it hardly matters, because now the managers have identified a reason to move on to something new. In this view, there is nothing funny about institutional fads. Rather, such

OFFICE FOLKLORE'S COMIC VIEW OF FAILURE

International Rowing Competition

The American rowing team and the Japanese rowing team had a race. The Japanese team won by a mile! The American team became very discouraged by the loss and began to sag. Corporate management decided the reason for the crushing defeat had to be found. They established a continuous improvement team to investigate the problem and recommend the appropriate corrective action. The result showed that the Japanese had eight people rowing and one person steering, while the American team had one person rowing and eight people steering. The American corporate steering committee immediately hired a consulting firm to do a study on this management structure. After some time and millions of dollars, the consulting firm concluded that too many people were steering and not enough people were rowing. The American team's management structure was then totally reorganized. The reorganized structure included three steering directors, three steering managers, two steering supervisors, and one rower. Included in the reorganization plan was a new performance standard which gave empowerment and enrichment to the rower in order to develop in him the incentive to work harder. The next year, the Japanese team won by two miles. Humiliated, the American corporation laid off the rower. To cut costs, it sold all the paddles, cancelled the capital investments for new equipment, ceased development of a new canoe, gave a superior performance award to the consulting firm, and distributed the money saved as bonuses to the senior executives.

–Collected in 1994

Source: Dundes and Pagter (1996: 23).

fads show serious people making serious decisions, reacting as best they can to information about their changing environments. There is an alternative defense. It concedes that, yes, many fads don't provide the solutions they promise, while arguing that that isn't the point. Rather, people need to appreciate the emotional benefits of institutional fads. Fads break the routine, the boredom that can make institutions seem sterile. Fads offer a sense of drama; they shake things up, add excitement. They give those involved a new sense of purpose and enable them to demonstrate their commitment to progress, to doing more and doing it better. They provide people with new challenges, new goals, and fresh ideas, as well as inspiration and self-confidence. In some ways, institutional fads resemble the self-help industry, except that self-help programs promise to help individuals deal with personal issues, such as shyness or troubled relationships, while institutional fads promise to make institutions and those who work within them more effective. In this view, the fad's substance has little significance—it hardly matters what the fad is about, so long as it can be used to jump-start the institution. And if a fad eventually gets rejected, that too is relatively unimportant, because any fad can be replaced by some new novelty that can serve the same emotional ends. According to these defenders, fads seem silly only because we miss their real purpose—providing variety and excitement.

Fads' critics also deny that institutional fads are a laughing matter, but they see fads' impact in more tragic terms. It is easy to imagine that fads might harm different people in various ways. Don't adopters have their hopes raised, only to have them crushed? Don't adopters waste colossal amounts of time, money, and energy implementing innovations that they later shed?

Aren't the institution's clients—the patients, students, customers, and so on—jeopardized by these bad choices? Don't employees lose confidence in the managers who make these bad choices, and isn't the result alienation, cynicism, and low morale? Don't fads distract us from real problems and real solutions? Aren't we rewarding promoters whose proposals are little better than the scams of confidence artists? This critical vision can be tailored to fit various ideological positions. For leftists, institutional fads can be seen as circuses put on to distract both an institution's members and the larger society from the appalling practices and failures of our institutions. For conservatives, fads reveal a troubling relativism, a readiness to continually shift our principles and practices. For rationalists, fads represent failures to evaluate evidence. Each of these critiques views fads as inefficient, wasteful.

Unfortunately, it is hard to assess the relative merits of these various positions. Are fads best understood as comic turns, wise decisions, morale boosters, or grim failures? For all that has been written about different institutional fads, commentators have paid remarkably little attention to their impact. Emerging and surging are exciting, heavily hyped processes, and analysts—just like the media and public attention—are drawn to study these visible, dramatic phases. In contrast, purging receives far less notice. People are often proud to be adopting a novelty because it demonstrates they are progressive and up-to-date. But they are much less inclined to publicize their decision to abandon a fad.[45] There are too many embarrassing interpretations. Did they make an unwise choice? Didn't they know what they were doing? Were they sufficiently prudent, or did they foolishly rush into something they didn't understand? Why couldn't they get the innovation to work? Don't they have the right stuff? It might not be so awkward if everyone knew about all of the other adopters bailing out; but if most of them keep quiet about their decisions to quit, people can be left with a sense that they have done something rather shameful. Because it is simply more difficult to learn about the process of purging, it is hard to evaluate the competing claims that institutional fads either boost morale and leave valuable sediments, or harm morale and leave behind wreckage.[46]

Part of our ignorance may derive from an understandable tendency to treat each institutional fad as unique. When people adopt a new diagnosis, teaching method, or management plan, they naturally focus on their good reasons for embracing that innovation; and if they later choose to abandon it, that decision, too, is seen as grounded in their direct experience with that particular novelty. But if we want to take a broader view, we need some way to move beyond the particulars of individual cases to examine more general patterns.

6

Fad Dynamics

Our oldest son started school when we lived in California. My wife and I enrolled Eric in a public school, and we attended the orientation program for parents of new students. The principal spoke. Among other things, she talked about how reading would be taught. The state of California, she said, had conducted an exhaustive review of the research literature on how children learn to read, and it had concluded that the most effective teaching method was whole language instruction. (*Whole language* was the current term for what had earlier been called *word recognition* or *sight reading;* that is, teaching based on the notion that children learn to read by becoming able to recognize different words in the context of what they're reading.)

Ten years later, had we still lived in California, and had we had another child starting school (we didn't, and we didn't), the principal's orientation speech would have been different. At that time, principals probably said something along these lines: drawing on (another) exhaustive review of the research literature on how children learn to read, the state of California had concluded that the preferred method of teaching reading was phonics.[1] (Phonics involves learning the sounds represented by the different letters, and then "sounding out" unfamiliar words.) In other words, within just a few years, the state's educational administrators had reversed themselves on their reading instruction policy.

How was this possible? People have been teaching children to read for a very long time—it's not as though they don't have plenty of experience in doing this. And psychologists and educators have been studying how students learn to read for a long time, too. It seems unlikely that some definitive research appeared during the ten-year period after Eric started school that proved the superiority of phonics. Moreover, as anyone who reads English knows full well, learning to read means *both* mastering the sounds made by the different letters (after all, phonics works pretty well most of the time) *and* learning to recognize words (because phonics doesn't work well for all English spellings). There may be some advanced rules of phonics that allow you to sound out *tough* (in which the letters *ough* sound like "uff"), *trough* (*ough* = "off"), *through* (*ough* = "ooo"), and *thorough* (*ough* = "oh"), but I don't know what they are—some words, most students just learn to recognize. It is curious that in spite of all the teachers' expertise, all the researchers' findings, and our collective personal experiences, people still manage to fight over how best to teach reading by insisting that we ought to emphasize one method over the other. Over time, expert opinion seems to have oscillated from favoring word recognition (a.k.a. sight reading, whole language) to phonics, then back again. My California example illustrates one of these shifts in the much longer history of reading instruction.

Is this sort of back-and-forth, pendulum-like oscillation typical? Do most institutional fads involve swinging back and forth between two poles (such as teaching students to recognize letters vs. teaching them to recognize words)? Or do other fads display different dynamics? This chapter examines some of the patterns by which fads come and go. We begin by considering some common images or metaphors—such as the pendulum—that we use to describe these processes. These images are important, because they shape how we think about fads. If we envision them in a particular way—say, in terms of a pendulum—this image can distort our understanding of how fads operate.

IMAGES OF CHANGE

Images of Progress: Arrows and Steps

The theme of progress—our sense that change is often for the better—occupies a central place in our culture. We often depict change using a very simple image—an arrow:

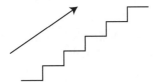

This image uses the flight of an arrow to suggest that changes involve movement in one direction: forward.[2] The arrow diagram suggests movement or change from one status, place, arrangement, or situation to another—from infant to adult, alcoholism to sobriety, and so on. There is, in this imagery, no notion of going back. In a slightly more complicated image, steps substitute for the arrow:

Images of steps or ladders offer even stronger suggestions of progress, in that climbing a set of steps implies—in addition to moving forward—rising, improving, getting better. This image also suggests that progress can be divided into distinct stages, that just as one step is clearly distinct from the next, so progress involves moving from one easily recognizable stage to the next. Thus, we distinguish between infants, toddlers, children, adolescents, and so on. Often, our institutions formally divide such stages into classes or ranks (preschool, elementary school, middle school, etc.), and may ceremonially mark the transition from one stage to the next (for example, with middle school graduation ceremonies). Very often, when proponents are extolling the promise of some innovation, they imply that adopting the novelty will produce not just change but a qualitative shift of this sort—an advance to a new and better stage or step.

Whether we envision change in terms of an arrow or climbing a set of steps, our notion of progress suggests that it is irreversible, that it involves moving in one direction—forward or, if you prefer, upward, never backward. One moves toward the future, and away from the past. Assuming that the current institutional fad represents this sort of onward-ever-onward progress is part of the illusion of diffusion.

Images of Oscillation: The Pendulum

But changes in the favored method of reading instruction haven't moved consistently forward; rather, they seem to swing back and forth, from teaching methods that emphasize phonics to methods that emphasize word recognition, and back again.

Here, the popular image is that of a pendulum, oscillating between two extremes:

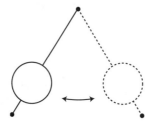

In the case of teaching reading, we might suspect that there is
a logical basis for these pendulum-like swings back and forth.
Learning to read involves recognizing combinations of *letters* as
words; that is, we might think of reading as requiring that students
master both of these components. Phonics, of course, emphasizes
letters, while word-recognition teaching methods emphasize
words. Let's say that at some historical moment, such as the year
our son Eric started school, whole language is the dominant
method used in California's schools. Inevitably, Californians will
discover that some children taught using that method are not
becoming good readers, that, in spite of our culture's perfection-
ist hopes, those children are being left behind. It is always possible for critics to argue that those poor readers are proof that what
we're doing to teach reading isn't working well enough, that we
need to try something different. Given the dual, learning letters/
learning words nature of reading, the easiest way of doing something different is to shift from emphasizing one to emphasizing
the other: thus, if we've been using whole language (and some

children aren't becoming good readers), let's shift to phonics. But this just sets up the next shift: soon critics will be able to point to children taught using the new method who continue to be left behind, and will call for another change: emphasizing phonics isn't working, so let's try word recognition methods. Because we always believe we could do better, we can always justify doing something different. Viewed this way, the pendulum swings don't seem that remarkable; our belief in perfectionism ensures that schools will always fall short and that critics can always call for changes, and there may be only one obvious alternative to current practices.

The pendulum image is a favorite of commentators who argue that such oscillating patterns characterize other institutional fads. For example, educational reforms are sometimes described as swinging from teacher-centered to student-centered policies.[3] Similarly, the history of experts' advice about child rearing has been categorized in terms of "parenting pendulum swings," from parent-centered to child-centered methods.[4] And the favored methods of management are said to oscillate back and forth between normative control (that is, emphasizing the manager's legitimate authority) and rational control (emphasizing efficiency), or between "top-down control" and "bottom-up empowerment."[5] These oscillations resemble the back-and-forth, pendulum-like findings in studies of clothing and grooming fashions. The length of women's skirts does not vary haphazardly from one year to the next; rather, skirts tend to rise for several years, then begin to fall for several more, before starting to rise again.[6] Similarly, the proportion of men who sport facial hair gradually rises for some span of years, before reversing and slowly falling.[7]

In short, observers often claim to detect back-and-forth, pendulum-like swings in fads. How should we make sense of these patterns? In thinking about what pendulum-like oscillations imply, we may find it helpful to consider our reading instruction example. The pendulum image requires a situation that people understand as having two opposing elements. Thus, reading instruction requires mastering both letters and words, so it is easy to think of instructional methods that emphasize instruction based on either letters or words. While it might be possible to devise reading instruction methods that have some other basis, just what that might involve isn't obvious. Similarly, there are practical limits to skirt lengths: skirts that are too long will drag on the ground, get filthy, and cause the wearer to stumble; skirts that are too short cannot provide the modest covering that is one of the principal purposes of any skirt.[8] Clearly, skirt lengths will vary within these limits. While there are many other dimensions along which skirts can vary (fullness, fabric, color, etc.), we tend to notice skirt length because it drastically affects how the wearer appears—her overall silhouette. This means that skirt length is a particularly obvious basis for characterizing complex, shifting fashions in dress.

In other words, we tend to use the pendulum image whenever we can characterize change as involving a single, readily apparent dimension with two opposing extremes (such as emphases on letters vs. words, or short skirts vs. long skirts), even though, if we think about it, we may realize that any change has many facets. Thus, classifying educational reforms as teacher-centered or student-centered, parenting as parent-centered or child-centered, or management as rational (more manager-centered) or normative (that is, more worker-centered) simplifies our thinking about schools, homes, and workplaces into settings

containing two sorts of people—teachers/students, parents/
children, managers/workers—and then argues that either one
element or the other of each pair must be emphasized. This is
actually a trick of classification. That is, an analyst can take a set
of seemingly different educational reforms, such as open classrooms, active learning, and so on, and argue that they all have
something in common—that is, they are all student-centered
rather than teacher-centered.

Noticing pendulum-like swings between student-centered
and teacher-centered reforms, then, simply requires that we decide to group all reforms into those two categories. The point is
not that it is wrong to conclude that some reforms are student-
centered, but that we could probably group educational reforms
into many categories, along many dimensions.[9] The pendulum
pattern we perceive simply reflects the way we've chosen to classify reforms. Note, too, that the pendulum image implies that an
institution's arrangements—like a pendulum—will return to the
same place. But surely this is too simple; education—like parenting, management, and other institutions—is evolving, so that
abandoning some fad doesn't mean that we return to exactly
where we were before we began.[10] The favored method of teaching may have oscillated between word recognition and phonics
methods over the years, but schools have changed in all sorts of
ways during that time.

Sometimes, it is much harder to classify innovations along a
single dimension. Consider dieting—a popular form of noninsti-
tutional fad. Nutritionists have been complaining about fad diets
for many decades.[11] Historically, most diet enthusiasms have
promised to promote good health, delay aging, or achieve moral
purity; it is only relatively recently that we have come to think of

dieting primarily in terms of weight loss. Still, there are all sorts of principles invoked as the basis for dieting to lose weight. These include calorie-based diets (which advocate weight loss through consuming fewer calories), low-fat diets (which emphasize the importance of cutting fat consumption), low-sugar diets, and low-carbohydrate diets, as well as all manner of all-the-grapefruit-you-can-eat diets. The point is, we generally don't think of diets as being divided between two rival master principles. Therefore, it is harder to envision dieting fads as swinging, pendulum-like, back and forth. Instead, fad diets seem to bounce about in all directions—moving more like a pinball than a pendulum.

Images of More Complex Patterns of Recurrence: The Wave and the Cycle

Perhaps more satisfactory images for such erratic shifts are the wave:

or the cycle:

The key feature of waves is their recurrence—one wave follows another. Each wave resembles, but is not exactly the same as, its predecessor—there is a trough, a swell, and a crest. Waves and cycles are similar images, in that they both illustrate a sequence of stages that, once completed, sets the conditions for its own repetition. I organized the discussion of institutional fads around one such image: the cycle of emerging, surging, and purging. While the sequence is standard—emerging always precedes surging, which in turn comes before purging—there is room for considerable variety. Some waves are bigger than others; particular waves can be affected by current conditions (akin to a gust of wind) or have unique elements.[12]

Compared to the constricted, back-and-forth motion of the pendulum, the wave image allows us more freedom to consider the complexity of institutional fads. Within any institution, say medicine, there are all sorts of possible bases of innovation—new diagnoses, new treatments, new specializations, new methods for organizing or managing hospitals, clinics, and care—too many dimensions to fit the pendulum image. Similarly, even if the pendulum is a reasonable image for thinking about reading instruction, there are many possible ways schools could change—what will be taught, how it will be taught, who will do the teaching, and on and on. There are always plenty of problems that people in institutions might like to solve, and there are always lots of folks who think they may know a better way of doing things. These ideas can come from all sorts of directions; there usually isn't just one dimension along which a pendulum swings back and forth (see box on pp. 140–141).

Still, we might ask why waves occur. If there are always problems and always people offering solutions, why do some of those solutions catch on, so that they surge into great visibility? Here, the media play a key role. Earlier, we recognized the media's great appetite for news; they need content—something they can report—and innovations, because they seem new and unfamiliar, are ideal for this purpose. At the same time, we need to appreciate the media's limited resources: newspapers can afford to print only so many column inches of news (the so-called news hole); there are only so many minutes available for broadcasters' programs, and only so many camera crews, reporters, and editors. Similarly, only one story can lead the broadcast or be featured on the magazine's cover. Thus, the media are continually sifting through potential topics, deciding which ones are most worthy of their coverage. Those decisions are made on lots of bases, but they have to be made.[13]

Timing matters. Imagine an innovation that its promoters hoped to launch in mid-September 2001. As we know, the September 11 terrorist attacks were a huge story, and they received unprecedented round-the-clock, commercial-free coverage for days. Though this intense level of coverage gradually receded, a large share of the media's attention was monopolized during the weeks that followed. Such big stories push lesser stories aside. It would have been easy to lose sight of any innovation introduced that fall. This is an extremely dramatic example, but it is important to realize that, on a lesser scale, similar considerations constantly affect all sorts of media coverage.

Thus, we might consider the media-hogging impact of a successful institutional fad. While it is surging—when this innovation is the focus of attention, with its book atop the best-

SKEPTICISM ABOUT WAVES OF MATH
INSTRUCTION REFORMS

Last week I got a burger at Burger King for $1.58. The counter girl took my $2 and was digging for my change when I pulled 8 cents out of my pocket and gave it to her. She stood there, holding the nickel and 3 pennies, while looking at the screen on her register.

I sensed her discomfort and tried to tell her to just give me back two quarters, but she hailed the manager for help and while he tried to explain the transaction to her, she stood there and cried. Why do I tell you this? Read on.

Teaching Math in 1950:

A logger sells a truckload of lumber for $100.
His cost of production is 4/5 of the price.
What is his profit?

Teaching Math in 1960:

A logger sells a truckload of lumber for $100.
His cost of production is 4/5 of the price, or $80.
What is his profit?

Teaching Math in 1970:

A logger exchanges a set "L" of lumber for a set "M"
   of money.
The cardinality of set "M" is 100. Each element is worth
   one dollar.
Make 100 dots representing the elements of the set "M."

(continued)

seller list, its promoters the subjects of magazine cover stories, and so on—it is difficult for other novelties to attract much notice. People, and particularly the media, are preoccupied with the current surge—it seems exciting, dramatic, and important, and fascination with it forces other would-be innova-

The set "C," the cost of production, contains 20 fewer points
than set "M."
Represent the set "C" as a subset of set "M."
Answer this question:
What is the cardinality of the set "P" of profits?

Teaching Math in 1980:
A logger sells a truckload of lumber for $100.
His cost of production is $80 and his profit is $20.
Your assignment:
Underline the number 20.

Teaching Math in 1990:
By cutting down beautiful forest trees, the logger makes $20.
What do you think of this way of making a living?
Topic for class participation after answering the question:
How did the forest birds and squirrels feel as the logger cut
down the trees?
There are no wrong answers.

Teaching Math in 2000:
A logger sells a truckload of lumber for $100.
His cost of production is $120. How does Arthur Andersen
determine that his profit margin is $60?

Teaching Math in 2005:
El hachero vende un camión carga por $100.
La costa de producción es . . .

— Humor circulating on the Internet

tions to the side. Once a wave is swelling, it is difficult to launch
another.

And yet, each wave must itself crest or peak, at least in its
media coverage. As time goes on, the surging innovation loses its
novelty and becomes familiar; news about it seems less fresh,

even stale. This is true both for fads and for innovations that become successful instances of diffusion. However marvelous television or polio vaccines (to name two tremendously successful innovations of the mid–twentieth century) may have seemed when they first appeared, they soon slipped off the front pages as they became standard, taken-for-granted aspects of life. No doubt every hometown newspaper had a photographer on hand to memorialize the first local kids lined up for their polio shots, but there was no point in continuing to take and print picture after picture as all the town's children were immunized. To be sure, the media will search for fresh angles for stories about whatever is surging, but, over time, these become ever harder to spot. Regardless of how successful the innovation may be, the media will find themselves looking for other stories. While it is hard for another topic to attract coverage when a big wave of coverage is swelling, gaining attention becomes much easier after the wave has broken.

In other words, the competition for media attention makes waves a likely pattern. Once a novelty's spread is noticed and the media begin to focus on it, there is a period when rival subjects have difficulty capturing media attention. But any story eventually becomes old, coverage tapers off, and new innovations are left with a better chance of moving into the limelight. The result is a pattern of successive waves in media coverage.

Images of Institutionalization: The Ratchet

I have argued that disappointment and boredom eventually spell the end of institutional fads. While this is generally true, there are exceptions—cases in which once an innovation is introduced, there seems to be no going back. That is, even if the change turns out to be flawed, the institution can't seem to shed it. Here, it may help to think about a different image—a ratchet:

Pendulums go back and forth, and waves rise and fall. In contrast, a ratchet permits easy movement in only one direction; efforts to reverse direction find that the mechanism is locked in place.

Change in some institutions resembles a ratchet, in that innovations, once introduced, are difficult to reverse.[14] Sometimes, for example, calls for change result in new laws, which are then hard to repeal. Here, we might consider the example of criminal penalties. In the 1980s, when concern about crack cocaine was at its height, the federal government passed new sentencing guidelines that set penalties for crack possession that were equivalent to those for possession of about 1/100th the amount of powdered cocaine.[15] The effects of equal amounts of the two drugs are about the same, yet possessing crack was treated as 100 times more serious an offense than possessing the same amount of powder. The law has racial consequences: African Americans are relatively more likely to be arrested for crack, and whites for powder; as a result, blacks receive stiffer sentences than whites for crimes that can be seen as equally serious. This troubling pattern has led to calls for reform, for reducing the penalties for crack so that they are equal to those for powdered cocaine; but lawmakers have proven reluctant to make these changes, because they don't want to go on record as reducing penalties for a drug that continues to have an especially bad reputation. It would probably be possible to pass even tougher penalties against crack, but it is very difficult to reduce the existing penalties, regardless of how problematic their consequences may be. This is the ratchet in action—or perhaps we should say inaction.

We can find plenty of other examples related to criminal justice. The widespread enthusiasm for boot camps led to their establishment in many states; the programs were retained, even after evaluation studies found that boot camps were no more effective in reducing recidivism than other correctional methods.[16] We have already seen (in chapter 5) how the DARE program continues, in the face of a good deal of evidence that suggests it isn't effective.

When it comes to dealing with drugs and crime, ratchetlike dynamics seem common. There is, of course, always more crime than we want—we'd prefer there to be none whatsoever. Perhaps the simplest, most easily understood approach to dealing with crime is to call for getting tougher: if we punish criminals more severely, the argument goes, fewer people will be willing to commit crimes and risk harsh sentences. Such arguments can be packaged in crowd-pleasing rhetoric—we need to get tough, crack down, no more slaps on the wrist, and so on. This means that it is relatively easy, particularly when fear of crime is widespread, to promote tougher measures, to ratchet up the penalties ever higher.[17] However, arguments that penalties are too high (for instance, that the sentencing guidelines for crack are too severe) encounter considerable resistance. Calls for their reduction run against the popular logic; surely, people assume, lighter penalties would invite more crime. Politicians are happy to vote for popular, get-tough measures, but they are reluctant to support reducing penalties and risk being labeled "soft on crime." Campaigns to reduce penalties encounter great resistance—just as a ratchet locks when pulled in the wrong direction.

To be sure, we can point to cases in which reformers have been able to reduce criminal penalties. Prohibition was repealed, and various states have at one time or another dropped the death penalty or reduced penalties for marijuana possession.[18] American history has been marked by waves of penal reforms intended to make imprisonment more humane, although these invariably find their limits—the public seems unwilling to support prison conditions that are more comfortable than the meanest standard of living found among citizens who are not incarcerated.[19] That is, prisons can never be made too comfortable ("country clubs"), and any reforms are hard-won—and easily lost if the tougher-punishment ratchet starts moving again.

The example of criminal justice, then, forces us to rethink the assumption that innovations can move freely back and forth (like a pendulum) or simply come and go (like a wave). In some circumstances, proposals that move in one direction, such as those to get tougher on crime, find much less resistance than calls to go the opposite way. Innovations—even those that seem ineffective—can become institutionalized. This is just another way that our simple images of change—arrows and steps, pendulums, and waves—ignore a good deal of complexity.

COMPLEXITY AND DIVERSITY

We almost always think about institutional fads one innovation at a time. Doing so makes it easier to understand the process. We isolate our attention on some instance of a novelty—open classrooms or cold fusion—and trace its path from emerging through surging and on to purging—the fad life cycle. These cycles occur, but we shouldn't forget that they occur within a broader context. Taking context into account complicates matters in at least three ways.

First, even within a single institution, few trends move everyone along at the same time and at the same pace. There probably has never been a year when all women's skirts were the same length, nor has there been a time when all businesses adopted the same management practices, or all teachers the same instructional methods. This is not just a matter of some people being trendsetters who climb aboard the bandwagon early, while the late adopters lag behind. Some people never adopt; they may oppose the change, be oblivious to the trend, or have their attention focused elsewhere. Not everyone shares the same concerns.

In complex, modern societies, diverse styles and tastes coexist. High schools offer a microcosm of these arrangements: high school students usually can choose among a set of identities— good students ("nerds" or whatever), good athletes ("jocks"), the disaffected ("stoners"), and so on. Similarly, they can declare preferences for musical genres, clothing styles, hairstyles, and slang. Often, we can spot patterns—youths with this identity tend to listen to that sort of music, wear these outfits, and use those words, although there are always individual exceptions who make unusual mixes of choices. Similar diversity can be found in the larger society, and innovations often spread first among those with particular identities or lifestyles before crossing over to other groups.[20] This tendency suggests that trends spread along our society's familiar fault lines. We're used to categorizing people by social class, race, gender, age, region, education, and so on. We are most likely to adopt innovations that others like us have already adopted (because we assume they probably have both similar tastes and similar needs); next, we favor the adoptions of those who are different but whom we want to emulate—perhaps because we want to become like them, perhaps because we figure they know things we don't know, or perhaps just because they so often seem to be trendsetters.

Much the same pattern exists within institutions. Among reading teachers, there are doubtless some strongly committed to emphasizing phonics, others equally committed to word recognition methods, and perhaps some who don't have a strong preference. Thus, the favored instructional method may vary from classroom to classroom, or (in schools where principals closely oversee what is taught) from one school to the next, or among districts that adopt different policies, and perhaps even from state to state. To be sure, when word recognition is ascendant, we can suspect that the pro-phonics teachers, schools, and districts may be more likely to keep their opinions to themselves, at least until word recognition seems to be slipping from favor. And conversely, when phonics is becoming increasingly visible, we can suspect that word recognition's advocates will teach more discreetly. Sociologists emphasize the pressures for conformity, and these certainly exist, but most large, complex institutions also have room for disagreement and diverse practices. Not everyone goes along with every trend (see box on p. 148).

**OFFICE FOLKLORE EXPRESSES DOUBTS
ABOUT THE FUTURE**

WE THE WILLING
LED BY THE UNKNOWING
ARE DOING THE IMPOSSIBLE
FOR THE UNGRATEFUL
WE HAVE DONE SO MUCH
FOR SO LONG
WITH SO LITTLE
WE ARE NOW QUALIFIED
TO DO ANYTHING
WITH NOTHING

—Versions in circulation since at least the 1970s
Source: Dundes and Pagter (1987: 95).

Second, there are often multiple innovations demanding
attention more or less simultaneously. A school principal's job is
multifaceted. The school has to decide how it will teach reading,
of course, but lots of other decisions have to be made as well.
How should arithmetic be taught, for example? What should the
school do about calls to teach—or not teach—sex education,
evolution, drug prevention, or bullying prevention? And there
are all those possible teaching methods—team teaching, block
scheduling, open classrooms, and so forth. The list goes on and
on. It's not as though reading instruction provides the basis for
the one institutional fad in schools. Instead, there are many
ongoing, competing institutional fads—some may be surging,
others purging; a particular school may ignore some of them,
dabble in others, and fully commit to only a few.

The result is considerable intra-institutional variation. The
frequency with which medical procedures occur—the number of

caesarean sections per thousand births, the percentage of children who have their tonsils removed—is known to vary a good deal from place to place.[21] We can imagine that while some births clearly require a C-section, and others just as clearly don't, some proportion will fall between these extremes and require judgment calls, for which some doctors will favor C-sections (that is, they will be relatively likely to operate in these ambiguous cases), and others will be much more reluctant to perform the surgery. Perhaps doctors with different preferences went to medical schools that taught different guidelines for operating. Perhaps the doctors are of different generations, and came of age during periods when the operation was either recommended or discouraged. Perhaps some insurance plans encourage or discourage the surgery. We can imagine all sorts of reasons why diverse preferences might coexist that account for variation in C-section rates from place to place. And remember, this is just one procedure—there will be similar variations in countless medical practices.

Talk of fads and fashions usually exaggerates their importance. "Everyone is wearing that style!" That's probably not true, unless we define *everyone* very narrowly. People dress—and teach reading, deliver babies, and manage businesses—in different ways. And while we may be able to trace the spread of a particular innovation, we shouldn't exaggerate its impact. Trends are rarely so all-encompassing as to override any diversity.[22]

Third, it is a mistake to assume that institutional fads have no lasting impact. When we speak of a fad having been purged, we imply that it has vanished, with no traces left behind. But this claim is too extreme. There may be a few people or organizations that cling to the fad, long after others have abandoned it. Even if most corporations dropped quality circles soon after adopting them, some firms may have found them useful, and continue using them. Often, adopting a fad requires that people learn new terms or new ways of doing things, and some may recall—and even use—certain of these teachings long after the fad has fallen from favor. Even the most faddish institutional fad is unlikely to disappear overnight.

In addition, institutional fads may be recalled as experiences. People who observed the methods used to get people charged up about some fad, later purged, now know some things about promoting other novelties. They may have opinions about what worked well and what wasn't so effective; and should they become enthusiastic about some new innovation, they will be better able to use what they learned to promote it more effectively. Similarly, the cynics—those who look back on yesterday's fad as a folly—can refer to their experiences ("I've seen 'em come, and I've seen 'em go") to justify their suspicions about today's novelty.

All of this suggests that such familiar images as the pendulum, the wave, and the cycle are flawed in that they assume that the course of every fad leads back to its starting place. Perhaps a more useful image is the spiral:

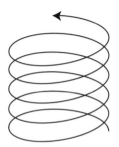

Like the cycle, the image of the spiral suggests that what goes around, comes around. But it also conveys a sense of change—the realization things never return to exactly where they began.[23] That is, the experience of having gone through an institutional fad—and perhaps even some of its ideas and practices—may be recalled, and this alters the conditions under which the next novelty will be considered.

In short, our images of fads—pendulums, waves, and ratchets—are too simple. They suggest a process in which people move if not in lockstep then at least along the same well-lit pathways. But the real world is far more complex. Whatever the trend, some people are deeply involved, but others have their attention focused elsewhere (perhaps on some very different development) or are oblivious to the changes that surround them. People discover and take many different routes, traveling toward a variety of destinations. The real world is in flux, filled with novelties that are having more or less success in capturing people's attention and allegiance.

Thinking about institutional fads, then, requires striking a balance between two contradictory ways of thinking about change. The first is to treat every innovation as unique. This is how promoters want us to think about their novelty: they want us to treat the change as the solution to some problem in education, medicine, or management; in particular, they don't want us to think of their novelty as just one more fad. The problem with this treat-each-innovation-as-unique approach is that it ignores the track record—the history of successive, forgotten management quality schemes, the oscillating shifts in reading instruction methods, and so on. These promoters ask us to forget that institutional fads occur.

The second way to think about changes is to assume that they follow completely predictable, repetitive patterns—as suggested in the popular images of the pendulum or the wave. The problem here is that this assumption ignores the real differences in the way fads evolve—and in their effects. Thinking about fad dynamics requires that we attend to both patterns and specifics. By doing so, we can become better prepared to respond to the claims about the next novelty.

7

Becoming Fad-Proof

Every institutional fad has boosters promoting its adoption. They promise change, transformation, progress, solutions to nagging problems, perhaps something approaching perfection. Sure, some of these promoters may be cynical hucksters, scamming the gullible with claims they know to be bogus; but many are completely sincere, dedicated converts convinced that their innovation offers the best route to a better future.

Of course, once the fad has run its course, those bright dreams become tarnished, the promises of great transformations lie in ruins, and the changes stand revealed as far less grand than once envisioned. What should we make of this wreckage?

We have already noted that those who backed adoption of some novelty that turns out to have been an institutional fad often are able to rationalize its failure. It could've, should've worked, they say, if only everyone had enlisted in the cause, gotten behind the change, provided the resources and commitment to make it work. This belief—"They never gave it a fighting chance!"—is one reason that some fads (such as methods of teaching reading) can reappear. Adherents of a failed fad can bide their time, waiting for a new opportunity to resurrect their solution to the institution's problems. For at least some loyalists, the fad failed not because it didn't work, but because the fainthearted gave up on it.

This is probably not the majority view. Most of us look back on discredited institutional fads and shake our heads—How could those people have been so foolish? To the degree that the fad consumed resources—budgets, people's time, and such—it now seems wasteful. If people were not only not helped but somehow actually harmed by the fad, the criticism is particularly harsh. Sometimes the failure is blamed on specific people who promoted adopting the fad within our organization; sometimes it is blamed on media hype, sometimes on the fad's originators. We might imagine that the result is fairly widespread disillusionment, cynicism, and damaged morale. Both the people working within an institution and those served by it may lose confidence in the institution's ability to do whatever it is supposed to do. Public opinion polls suggest that people's confidence in most institutions has declined since 1960. While we can't blame institutional fads for all of that decline, it seems unlikely that their failures do much to promote or restore confidence in our institutions.

This raises another set of questions: Are there things we can do to prevent the harms caused by institutional fads—ways of fad-proofing ourselves, and even our organizations and institutions? And, if so, is fad-proofing desirable?

GUIDELINES FOR FAD-PROOFING

Given what we know about the processes by which institutional fads spread, we can devise some guidelines for fad-proofing.

1. Don't forget what happened last time. Institutional fads cannot occur on their own. They require favorable conditions: a culture that believes in progress, media that publicize whatever's new, and so on. Modern conditions favor the diffusion of innovations; they made it possible for personal computers and cell phones to catch on with astonishing speed. But the presence of conditions that sometimes encourage the spread of incredibly useful innovations does not mean that all novelties can live up to their promoters' promises. Most institutional fads fail because they turned out to be bad ideas, or at least they weren't nearly so good as their advance billing promised.

People tend to focus on institutional fads one at a time, as though each stands apart from all the others. This is understandable. After all, when promoters draw our attention to a particular innovation, they invite us to think about the specific improvements that this change promises to bring—we concentrate on those claims. But viewing each innovation as unique misses the larger pattern, the way heavily hyped novelties rise—and then collapse—one after another. This book has argued that our society is vulnerable to institutional fads, to short-term enthusiasms for solutions to our many problems. Even the smartest people, concerned about the most serious problems, can and do succumb to promoters' promises. Once we recognize institutional fads as characteristic of our culture, once we acknowledge that there already have been many such fads and that we are vulnerable to others in the future, it becomes reasonable to ask questions when a new innovation comes on the scene, to check to see whether this novelty bears the hallmarks of an institutional fad.

2. Be skeptical about astonishing claims. Announcements that there is some new new thing that will transform an established institution need to be approached critically. There are obvious questions to ask. Why, if this is such a terrific idea, haven't people thought of it before? (Or, if the idea has been around for a while, why haven't they been using it?) What evidence do we have that this innovation will actually work and—very importantly—is there any evidence suggesting that it might not work? Do we have any estimates for what the change is expected to cost, and for the value of the expected benefits—and what is the basis for those estimates? There is nothing wrong with posing such questions. Remember, the burden of proof ought to be on those making the claims: the promoters ought to be able to make a convincing case that whatever change they're advocating is worthwhile; it isn't up to the skeptics to prove that there is something wrong with the innovation.

3. Continue to insist on persuasive evidence. The longer an innovation has been around, the more evidence ought to be available regarding its effectiveness. In its early stages, an innovation's advocates probably have little more than a theory—this is how we believe this innovation will work and why we think it will work this way. A little later, they may be able to report anecdotal evidence—when this company or campus or clinic adopted this innovation, they experienced some success. Often these anecdotes are summarized along the lines of "Organization X's recent success suggests that . . . ," "Early indications are that . . . ," or "Experts hope that . . ." Note that the media tend to be quite willing to present this sort of evidence, because it can be presented as pathbreaking news, and thus makes their reports seem more dramatic. However, it is also important to realize that a favorable anecdote or comments about early indications or hopes do not constitute particularly strong evidence. People who adopt innovations on the basis of this sort of flimsy support need to realize that there is every reason to doubt that their expectations will be fulfilled. In particular, those who are relatively late in adopting an innovation ought to insist on more and better evidence of the innovation's worth than what those who preceded them received.

This means that it is vital to keep an eye on how innovations actually perform. Ideally, doing so involves keeping track of two different developments. The first is external. If others have adopted the innovation, then as time goes on, there should be more and more evidence emerging about just how things are going. Here, we should watch not for upbeat, self-serving press releases but for studies that actually test the innovation's effectiveness. It is essential that these tests be designed so that they can reveal failure as well as success. They should, at a minimum, involve comparisons between those who have adopted the innovation and those who have forgone that opportunity—that is, a good test ought to involve some sort of control group (and the more sophisticated the comparisons between the adopters and the control group, the better the test). Such comparisons enable us to see that either yes, those who adopted the innovation performed better than the control group, or no, the adopters' performance was no better (or perhaps even worse!) than the control group's.

Such research takes time. It may take years to discover whether a new method of teaching reading, a new drug-prevention program, or a new medical treatment is in fact superior to what we've been doing. Moreover, the earliest studies to appear probably will have more design flaws than those that follow, so that promising early research results may prove to have been too optimistic.[1] However, anyone thinking about investing their time and money in an innovation ought to be interested in watching for and evaluating the evidence of its worth. Contradictory results from different studies should be viewed not as annoying inconsistencies but as important warning signs: What might account for those different results? And, if no stronger evidence appears as time passes, that in itself is important information. Why, if the innovation works so well, aren't its advocates able to provide ever better evidence of its effectiveness?[2]

The second set of developments is internal. If your organization has adopted a new management style, you need to assess how well it is working for you. Again, evidence can take different forms and be more or less useful. Early in the adoption process, there is an almost inevitable tendency to measure the extent of adoption—this many people have attended the training workshops, this many units have had people certified in the new procedures, this many reports are now in the new format, and so on. Such measures are necessary—somebody has to make sure that the adoption is actually occurring—but it is important to remember that this sort of information about the novelty's spread tells you nothing whatsoever about whether the innovation is proving valuable. Nor will firsthand testimonies of people within the organization necessarily be of much value—they may be caught up in the excitement of doing something different, or trying to curry favor by saying what they think their bosses want to hear. Over time, the organization ought to be able to measure some effects (higher profits, increased efficiency, or whatever). In other words, there ought to be evidence that some things have actually changed—and that these changes can be traced to the innovation's improving the organization's effectiveness.

4. Don't focus on the fear of being left behind. Evidence is important, and the greater the risk, the more important having good evidence ought to be in deciding whether to take that risk. After all, the more it will cost to adopt the innovation, the more you'll lose if it doesn't work. Many people and organizations rush to join institutional fads because they fear losing out if they wait too long. What will happen, they worry, if all our competitors adopt the new method and suddenly become much more successful, while we lag behind? Sure, that's a consideration. But it has a flip side: What do we stand to lose if we invest heavily in this innovation and it doesn't work any better than what we're already doing? When they focus too much on the potential gains that adoption might bring, people wind up downplaying the potential costs. Similarly, concentrating on the imagined costs of being left behind ignores the possibility that delaying adoption will prove less costly if the fad turns out to be a bust.

This sort of calculus accounts for much of the appeal of unorthodox medical treatments. These tend to flourish for two sorts of ailments for which conventional medicine cannot promise much hope: chronic conditions (such as arthritis) and incurable diseases (such as terminal cancer). In these cases, some patients feel they have nothing to lose—they have exhausted conventional medicine's techniques and found them inadequate, and they reason that they might as well try whatever alternative treatments promise relief.[3]

But most institutional fads occur not because people believe they can't lose, but because they focus narrowly on the possible costs of failing to adopt a worthwhile innovation. Expanding their scope of vision to encompass *both* the costs and benefits of *both* adopting and not adopting might slow their rush to enlist in some dubious new trend.

5. Remember: people rarely proclaim their disappointments. Institutional fads begin with bright hopes and great optimism; the adoption of the innovation tends to be announced with public fanfare. In contrast, disillusionment and the abandonment of novelties that aren't working well tend to be much quieter processes; nobody wants to publicize their mistakes. Others aren't likely to broadcast their decisions to climb off the bandwagon. You need to pay attention, to be alert for the signs of bad news. If somebody eventually whispers that the emperor is naked, you need to be listening.

THE PROMISE OF CHANGE

Because our culture believes in progress, we worship change. We often ridicule those who are suspicious of change, afraid to change, slow to change. They are suspected of somehow endorsing—perhaps profiting from—the flaws in the status quo. They are seen as unimaginative, unable to grasp the opportunities that the future holds. This critique is easy to apply at many levels. Long after my wife and our sons had cell phones, I remained phone-less (or, as I preferred to think of it, phone-free), and I received a fair amount of razzing about my failure to get with it. Similarly, converts to any new belief smile and shake their heads at those who still refuse to accept feng shui, neoconservatism, Area 51, low-carb diets, the postmodernist paradigm, or whatever. Refusing to climb aboard the bandwagon looks—to those already onboard—shortsighted and foolish. It calls to mind those small-minded fools who laughed at the Wright brothers or insisted that rock and roll wouldn't last. This criticism offers comfort to those who have adopted whatever innovation is at question—they can congratulate themselves on being farsighted, progressive, bold, on the cutting edge, and so on.

We should not underestimate the power of these opinions. We do not live in a society that expects stability, that believes things will remain the same. We have seen our world change, and we have heard our parents and grandparents describe even greater changes. Every shift is welcomed by some and rejected by others, and it is easy to look back and make fun of those who resisted what would prove to be enduring changes. They look foolish to us, and we don't want to look foolish to those who follow. Worse, some of those people were resisting causes that we now see as having been right or just, and we don't want to resist changes that will lead to a better world. It is easy to get caught up in wanting to be part of the march of progress.

However, being open to change does not require that we rush to embrace every novelty. Lots of fads are inconsequential and don't cost all that much. You need a refrigerator, but its color doesn't affect its ability to keep food cold. Still, manufacturers have discovered that people will replace working appliances to get one in a currently desirable color (remember when harvest gold and avocado were popular?). Similarly, you may get rid of clothing before it wears out, simply because it no longer seems fashionable. But you probably consider those costs to be manageable, and they may be offset by the satisfactions of having a stylish kitchen or wearing something different.[4]

Institutional fads are different. They often cost much more to adopt (a corporation may spend millions implementing some new management approach), and the potential costs of failure are greater. How much risk is acceptable if we're talking about the chances that your children's school's reading instruction program won't work well? How much risk is acceptable if we're talking about the effectiveness of the medical treatments given to your family members? How much money do you want to invest in companies that spend millions on unproven management schemes? Modern life requires that much of the time, we place our affairs in the hands of people who presumably know what they're doing. Most of us want to believe that our kids' teachers, our doctors, our bosses, and the managers of the companies in our portfolios will make wise choices. We assume that they'll keep up (that is, make the changes that should be made), but we're also counting on them not to be duped by every novelty featured in the media.

Talking about the march of progress implies that change occurs at a steady pace, and always moves forward. That's wrong. Change is messy. It involves lots of false starts, uncertainty, and confusion. Sometimes, people make unwise choices—they guess wrong about how things will change, and they scramble aboard bandwagons headed nowhere.

There has to be a middle path between refusing to change and seizing on every novelty that becomes available. Being aware that institutional fads are common and demanding to assess the evidence before joining the crowd are vital to discovering that path.

Notes

1. The Illusion of Diffusion

1. Hula hoops are discussed in Hoffmann and Bailey (1991: 185–87), Johnson (1985: 41–45), and Marum and Parise (1984: 104–5).

2. Studies of fads often present graphs of this shape. See, for example, E. Abrahamson and Fairchild (1999: 721); Aguirre, Quarantelli, and Mendoza (1988: 578); John Gill and Whittle (1992: 289); Kieser (1997:51); Placier (1996: 245).

3. Most popular books about fads present catalogs of such playful, largely forgotten enthusiasms: Hoffmann and Bailey (1990, 1991, 1992, 1994); Hoffmann and Manning (2002); Johnson (1985); Kirchner (1995); Marum and Parise (1984); Panati (1991); Smith and Kiger (2004).

4. Barnett (1995); Hoffmann and Bailey (1991).

5. There are no general discussions of institutional fads, but analysts have written explicitly about fads in specific institutions. The largest literature concerns management fads (often dignified by the label *fashion*) in business; see, for example, E. Abrahamson and Fairchild (1999); Brindle and Stearns (2001); Cole (1999); Jackson (2001). At least in an earlier age, educators felt free to speak of educational fads (H. Buchholz 1931; Knight 1948; Redway 1896). Contemporary educators are more likely to speak of a succession of short-lived "reforms"; see, for example,

Cuban (1990); Ravitch (2000); Sarason (1996). Higher education management's fads have also attracted analysts' attention (Birnbaum 2000; Stensaker 1998). Studies of academic and scientific fads include W. Abrahamson, Whitman, and Price (1989); Aguirre (2002); Bronfenbrenner (1966); Crane (1969); Fell (1960); Hagstrom (1965); Peng (1994); Powell (1968); and Silverman (2000). The medical literature tends to avoid speaking of either fads or fashion, but see Black (1999); Blumberg (1999); Burnum (1987); Campbell and Johnson (1999); Silverstein (1997).

6. Bogardus (1924). He continued this research for decades; see Bogardus (1950: 305–9).

7. *New York Times* (1915: 9).

8. On the spread of the male wedding ring, see Howard (2003). Steinberg (2004) illustrates the reverse process—the demise of men's hats.

9. For reviews of the diffusion literature, see Rogers (1995); Wejnert (2002).

10. Mulligan (2004).

11. For example, Rolf Meyersohn and Elihu Katz (1957: 594 n. 1) "choose to ignore the distinction between the two concepts." The anthropologist Edward Sapir (1931: 139) argued that compared to fashion, a fad has narrower appeal, shorter duration, and "always differs from a true fashion in having something unexpected, irresponsible or bizarre about it." For Erich Goode (1992: 350), "a fad . . . is temporary . . . and . . . trifling or insignificant. . . . [Fashion] applies to a broader range of activities and phenomena." David Miller (2000: 182) suggests instead that "fads are less predictable, and their life cycles shorter and more intense [and] . . . more trivial than fashion. . . . Fashion usually communicates economic status more clearly than fads [and] . . . some have argued that fashion is more enduring." John Lofland (1990: 445) emphasizes fads' emotional aspect: "A fad is an amusing mass involvement. . . . Words often associated with the term include: madcap, hijinks, antics, lark, silly, funny." There is, in short, no consensus about the difference between the two concepts.

12. For a classic description of this trickle-down system, see Barber

and Lobel (1952). There are many sociological interpretations of haute couture fashion; for example, see Crane (2000); Davis (1992); Finkelstein (1998). Of course, globalization and other social changes have transformed the fashion world, and diminished Parisian power in the process.

13. Simmel ([1904] 1957). While Simmel was not the first to observe that fashions tend to move down the status hierarchy, his is the analysis that sociologists tend to cite; Carter (2003) discusses some earlier fashion theorists.

14. For observations about the fluid relationship between status and contemporary trendsetting, see Crane (2000); Field (1970); Gladwell (2000); Suzuki and Best (2003); T. Wolfe (1968, 1970).

15. Epstein (2002: 172).

16. Hirsch (1972).

17. Hayes and Bing (2004) describe the uncertain process of promoting movies.

18. Herbert Blumer (1969) saw this uncertainty as the central feature of fashion; he argued that fashions are products of *collective selection*, in which many people come to agree on particular choices.

19. We might think of there being niches or markets for campus fads, toy fads, and other fad clusters—places in society where conditions make it easy for fads to emerge and spread. College campuses, for instance, feature relatively homogeneous populations, with substantial amounts of free time and under modest supervision, and a culture of competition among groups both within each campus and among campuses (Aguirre, Quarantelli, and Mendoza 1988). Such conditions may encourage the spread of fads (see also McPhail 2005).

20. On toys as a culture industry, see Stern and Schoenhaus (1990).

21. Hacking (1995); McHugh (1992); Mulhern (1991).

22. E. Abrahamson and Fairchild (1999, 2001); Cole (1999); Lawler and Mohrman (1985); Zeitz, Mittal, and McAulay (1999).

23. Huizenga (1992); Mellican (1992); B. Simon (2002).

24. John Gill and Whittle (1992: 282) make the cycle explicit: "managerial activity . . . seems to proceed from deep disillusionment with one panacea that has run its course to high enthusiasm for the next."

25. E. Abrahamson and Fairchild (1999: 709) speak of "constant transience."

2. Why We Embrace Novelties

1. On the history of educational reforms, see Ravitch (2000); Sarason (1996); Tyack and Cuban (1995).

2. Thus, analysts have described management fads in several European countries and Japan: see Benders and van Veen (2001); Brindle and Stearns (2001); Furusten (1999); Hamde (2002); Jackson (2001); Kieser (1997). For discussions of how institutional fads in the United States can affect nations around the world, see J. Meyer (2004); Naim (2000); Walt (2000).

3. There is a large popular literature about the challenges posed by change. For example, Alvin Toffler's 1970 best-seller, *Future Shock*, classified three dimensions of change: transience (arrangements don't last as long as they used to), novelty (unfamiliar developments emerge), and diversity (there are more options to choose among). Other examples of the genre include T. Buchholz (1999), Dychtwald and Flower (1990), and Peterson (2000).

4. Brindle and Stearns (2001).

5. Nisbet (1980) traces the intellectual history of progress.

6. Lasch (1991) shows that these concerns have long been part of American thought.

7. Herman (1997) offers a history of fears about decline.

8. On Americans' reluctance to acknowledge progress, see Best (2001); Easterbrook (2003).

9. Easterbrook (2003: 84) calls this continuing need for change the "unsettled character of progress."

10. E. Abrahamson (1996a: 257).

11. On intractability, see Sarason (1990).

12. Brindle and Stearns (2001); Sterman and Wittenberg (1999).

13. One recent compendium's title—*Forgotten Fads and Fabulous*

Flops—emphasizes the precarious, transitory nature of many enthusiasms (Kirchner 1995). Prognostications about the impact of innovations are often wildly wrong; see, for example, Corn (1986). On the place of failure in American culture, see Sandage (2005).

14. On the importance of the idea of revolution in marketing, see Frank (1997).

15. Kuhn (1962).

16. There are other breakthrough synonyms: "Proponents . . . argue that the implementation of [Business Process Reengineering] ideas involve a *major departure* from current practices, which therefore demands *radical, rather than incremental, change,* in order to ensure the '*order-of-magnitude improvements*' " (Newell, Swan, and Robertson 1998: 300; emphasis added).

17. For recent explorations of these themes, see B. Lewis (2002); Macfarlane and Martin (2002).

18. Fineman (2001).

19. E. Abrahamson (1991, 1996b); J. Meyer and Rowan (1977). Economics postulates that people make rational choices, based on their calculations of costs and benefits, and economic models shape decision making in many institutions (E. Abrahamson and Rosenkopf 1993).

20. Eric Abrahamson (1991: 589) calls this "proinnovation bias."

21. Cuban (1990); Sarason (1996); Tyack and Cuban (1995).

22. The great German sociologist Max Weber (1946) identified a parallel process operating among individuals. He suggested that democracy and social fluidity encouraged a sensitivity to fashion.

23. Sociologists call these similarities *institutional isomorphism*. For the classic discussion, see DiMaggio and Powell (1983). Zorn (2004) offers a case study—corporations creating a position of chief financial officer.

24. Sociologists emphasize the importance of connections that link otherwise separate networks (variously described as having "weak ties" or being "loosely coupled") in spreading information (Granovetter 1973; Weick 1976).

25. On globalization and diffusion, see Walt (2000); Wejnert (2002).

26. Aguirre (2002).
27. Wejnert (2002).

3. The Fad Cycle: Emerging

1. Quotes from J. Mathews and Katel (1992: 48); Shao (1995: A121); Stewart (1993: 41). On the general quest for quality in business, see Cole (1999).

2. Aronowitz (1998); Richman and Jason (2001); Showalter (1997). For other examples of faddish diagnoses of ambiguous medical conditions, see Burnum (1987); Silverstein (1997).

3. Hagstrom (1965) notes that scientists see their work as solving problems, but that while some sciences are characterized by consensus regarding what are the key intellectual puzzles, others feature more disagreement. He argues that the former are less susceptible to fashions in choosing research topics.

4. Or, more formally: "Organizational members encounter [demand-side] cues or 'issues' . . . indicating that the organization needs to change" (Zbaracki 1998: 613).

5. The sociologists who have given the most attention to this process are analysts of social problems who try to explain how and why particular issues become public concerns. They argue that someone must make claims that bring a social problem to others' attention by explaining what is wrong (this is sometimes called a *diagnostic frame*). For an introduction to this literature, see Loseke (2003).

6. Placier (1996).

7. Not everyone has to endorse the new solution. Wilsnack (1979) notes that many proposed changes inspire opposition in the form of *counterfads*—campaigns that challenge whatever changes are being proposed. This opposition may be rooted in various interests (experts who debunk what they view as specious claims, people who hope to preserve or restore some way of life, etc.), but they resist either the claim that

there is a problem or the argument that the proposed solution will solve it.

8. Hamde (2002). Gibelman (2004) argues that disenchantment with existing social welfare services leads to a constant search for new providers.

9. Lemann (1997); P. Wolfe and Poynor (2001).

10. Kieser (1997). Of course the explanations favored by professionals tend to be much more technical and complex than the versions disseminated to the public.

11. Note that such successes don't prove much. Sterman and Wittenberg (1999: 337) observe, "Even in cases where the ideas of the [management] guru have little merit, the energy and enthusiasm a team can bring to bear on a problem, coupled with Hawthorne and placebo effects and the existence of 'low hanging fruit,' will often lead to some successes, both real and apparent. Proponents rapidly attribute these successes to the use of the guru's ideas."

12. Park (2000). For other examples of scientists relaxing their standards for evidence and, as a result, wandering down false paths, see Gardner (1957); Langmuir (1953).

13. Blumer (1969: 286–87) specifies the conditions required for fashion to flourish. They include the following: "there must be a relatively free opportunity for choice between the models [i.e., the available options]"; and "the pretended merit or value of the competing models cannot be demonstrated through open and decisive test. . . . [F]ashion does not take root in those areas of utility, technology, or science where the asserted claims can be brought before the bar of demonstrable proof. In contrast, the absence of means for testing effectively opens the door to other considerations in making choices between them." On bandwagon discourse, see E. Abrahamson and Fairchild (1999).

14. For example, see Clark and Salaman (1996); Huczynski (1993); Micklethwait and Wooldridge (1996).

15. Huczynski (1993: 42). In contrast, more skeptical critics refer to *alchemists*, *charlatans*, or *voodoo* (Kieser 1997).

16. E. Abrahamson and Fairchild (2001: 154).

17. Clark and Salaman (1996: 87).

18. Brunsma (2004); Cohn (1996); Hoffler-Riddick and Lassiter (1996); Loesch (1995).

19. Tyack and Cuban (1995: 55).

20. Aguirre (2002).

21. D. Collins (2003: 194). Strang and Meyer (1993) argue that diffusion is most successful when it involves theorization (i.e., abstract ideas that can be applied in many contexts), rather than more concrete specifics that may fit only particular settings. For an example of how abstraction enhanced the dissemination of one scholar's ideas among academics, see Lamont (1987).

22. Benders and van Veen (2001) call this ambiguity in the presentation of solutions "interpretive viability."

23. E. Abrahamson (1996b).

24. Ingersoll (2003) points out the different ways that competing ideologies account for schools' failings.

25. On the broad appeal of educational reforms, see Tyack and Cuban (1995: 45).

26. On this tendency, see Fineman (2001); John Gill and Whittle (1992).

27. See, for example, Lutz (1996).

28. Again, Blumer (1969: 287) notes that fashion requires "the presence of prestige figures who espouse one or another of the competing models." The high-status connection may be to "other recent fashions or approaches, providing *legitimacy by association*" (Fineman 2001: 21; emphasis in original).

29. Soule (1999) describes how media coverage fostered the spread of an ineffective protest tactic.

30. Benders and van Veen (2001).

31. Gladwell (2000); Granovetter (1973); Newell, Swan, and Robertson (1998).

32. Again, the sociological term for this is *institutional isomorphism* (DiMaggio and Powell 1983).

33. For a case study of this tendency, see Placier, Walker, and Foster (2002).

34. Birnbaum (2000). Similarly, Tyack and Cuban (1995: 112) argue that school administrators follow management fads.

35. Huczynski (1993) and Micklethwait and Wooldridge (1996) discuss diffusion to the United States. Not surprisingly, Walt (2000) suggests that cross-national diffusion is easier when ideas are abstract, and when countries belong to the same networks and view themselves as similar.

36. The media contribute to shifting evaluations of status by regularly ranking the top graduate programs, the best corporations to work for, top-earning growth funds during the past quarter, and countless other intra-institutional comparisons. To the degree that they are thought to influence prospective students, investors, and so on, these rankings encourage firms to compare themselves to the leaders, and—on the assumption that the leaders' high status is somehow due to whatever they're doing—to try to follow those leaders.

37. Glaberson (1995); Micklethwait and Wooldridge (1996).

38. Scheirer (1990).

39. Glazer (2000).

40. E. Abrahamson (1991).

41. Katz and Lazarsfeld (1955); Rogers (1995).

42. E. Abrahamson (1996b); Suzuki and Best (2003).

43. Carson et al. (1999) and Gibson and Tesone (2001) suggest that the firms that are most likely to adopt management fads are those that have adopted—and abandoned—previous fads.

44. E. Abrahamson and Fairchild (1999, 2001); Westphal, Gulati, and Shortell (1997); Zbaracki (1998); Zeitz, Mittal, and McAulay (1999).

45. Blumer (1969). See also E. Abrahamson (1996a).

46. Lofland (1993: 227), in trying to explain why particular social movements take off, speaks of "the Darwinian parade of proposers."

47. On the diffusion of medical treatments in the absence of much research documenting their effectiveness, see Burnum (1987); Mapes (1977); Robin (1985).

48. E. Abrahamson and Fairchild (1999, 2001); Aldag (1997); Kieser (1997); Westphal, Gulati, and Shortell (1997). In sharp contrast to these other authorities, Furnham (2004: 3) insists that many management fads begin with an "academic discovery."

49. Brindle and Stearns (2001).

50. "For many management theorists, books are largely a form of advertising for even more profitable activities" (Micklethwait and Wooldridge 1996: 47). See also D. Collins (2003).

51. Clark and Greatbatch (2004: 409, 411). See also Clark (2004); Furusten (1999).

52. Clark and Greatbatch (2004: 409).

53. E. Abrahamson and Fairchild (1999); Kieser (1997).

54. E. Abrahamson and Fairchild (2001).

55. Goffman (1959).

4. The Fad Cycle: Surging

1. On low-carb eating, see Boyle (2004); Yonan (2005). On diet fads generally, see Barnett (1995); Fumento (1997); McHenry (1960).

2. Aguirre (2002: 103, 106).

3. Chancellor (1999); Galbraith (1990); Kindleberger (1978); Shiller (2000). For an analysis of how the press often interprets market fluctuations in emotional terms, see Warner and Molotch (1993). For a detailed analysis of the most recent bull market (1982–99), see Mahar (2003).

4. On surging, see Aguirre (2002); Lofland (1993). On momentum, see Adler (1981). Lofland's (1990) classification of collective behavior by the dominant emotion associated with different forms links fads to joy.

5. Clark and Greatbatch (2004); Greatbatch and Clark (2003); Huczynski (1993).

6. On boredom as a psychological state that makes business leaders welcome management fads simply because they involve change, see E. Abrahamson (1996a, 1996b); Huczynski (1993).

7. Sommer (1974).

8. Brindle and Stearns (2000); Huczynski (1993). On status seeking as a motivation behind institutional fads, see E. Abrahamson (1996a, 1996b). There have been many efforts to understand style and taste as social phenomena; see, for instance, Bourdieu (1984); Postrel (2003).

9. Soule (1999) describes activists adopting a protest style that, while ineffective, matched their assumptions about effective tactics. This case should remind us that adopters are selective; they can and do reject many more novelties than they select.

10. Kieser (1997).

11. Economists argue that fads can be understood as *information cascades*; that is, learning that some people have adopted a novelty creates pressure on others to follow suit—and the larger the number of perceived adopters, the greater the pressure (Bikhchandani, Hirshleifer, and Welch 1992, 1998; Hirshleifer 1995). For an example of media publicity about others' choices spreading a fad, see Aguirre, Quarantelli, and Mendoza (1988). On the process in education, see Slavin (1989).

12. Placier, Walker, and Foster (2002).

13. Aguirre, Quarantelli, and Mendoza (1988).

14. Robin (1984) argues that fear of lagging behind medicine's cutting edge accounts for doctors who join iatroepidemics (that is, the spread of harmful medical practices).

15. E. Abrahamson (1996b).

16. Durkheim (1982).

17. E. Abrahamson and Rosenkopf (1993) refer to these as "institutional pressures" and "competitive pressures," respectively.

18. Other pioneers have already blazed this particular trail. Remember that the physicist Alan Sokal succeeded in publishing scientific gibberish in one literary journal (Guillory 2002). For examples of careerist motives for joining academic fads, see Fell (1960); Peng (1994). For a general theory of the evolution of academic discourse, see Abbott (2001).

19. Placier (1996).

20. Huczynski (1993: 281) notes that management fads can be a "career enhancer." See also Brindle and Stearns (2000).

21. Strang and Macy (2001). Khurana (2002) offers a case study of the way this thinking has been personalized: in recent years, the business world has shown enthusiasm for hiring charismatic CEOs who are presumed to have personal qualities that can solve a corporation's problems.

22. John Gill and Whittle (1992).

23. Rogers (1995).

24. Rogers (1995: 265–66).

25. Brunsma (2004: 103) notes that "It is excruciatingly difficult to obtain data regarding the number of schools and districts that have dropped their [school] uniform policies. . . . [T]he media are not covering policies that have failed."

26. Malmi (1999); Westphal, Gulati, and Shortell (1997).

27. Birnbaum (2000: 133) refers to this as "culture lag" between organizational sectors.

28. Jackson (2001: 16) argues that management gurus have inspired a "backlash."

29. Dundes and Pagter have published several collections, each offering hundreds of examples (e.g., 1975, 1987, 1996, 2000).

30. Books by *Dilbert*'s creator, Scott Adams, have also become successful (and are sometimes included on lists of best-selling management books).

31. Stensaker (1998).

32. Becker (1995); Hannan and Freeman (1984). The symphony example that follows in the paragraph is Becker's.

5. The Fad Cycle: Purging

1. For a critical history of the enthusiasm for bone marrow transplants in treating breast cancer, see Welch and Mogielnicki (2002). Of course, medicine is not always so responsive to scientific evidence. For arguments that medicine can ignore or give insufficient weight to such evidence, see Campbell and Johnson (1999); Lipton and Hershaft (1985); Mapes (1977); McDonald (1996); Robin (1984).

2. In contrast, studies of diffusion tend to equate innovations with progress; novelties that prove ineffective or temporary are even labeled "mistakes" (Soule 1999).

3. For example, see Ennett et al. (1994); Wysong, Aniskiewicz, and Wright (1994).

4. Wysong, Aniskiewicz, and Wright (1994: 464).

5. Recall Blumer's (1969: 286–87) argument: "Fashion is not guided by utilitarian or rational considerations. . . . [T]he pretended merit or value of the competing models cannot be demonstrated through open and decisive test. . . . [F]ashion does not take root in those areas of utility, technology, or science where asserted claims can be brought before the bar of demonstrable proof."

6. For studies showing some scientists clinging to ideas most of their colleagues have abandoned, see H. Collins (2000); Simon (2002).

7. For example, Sarason (1996) argues that educational reforms are often able to avoid independent evaluations with research designs that might identify their failings.

8. E. Abrahamson and Fairchild (1999); Spell (1999, 2001).

9. Newell, Swan, and Robertson (1998).

10. Jenness and Grattet (2001). Best (1999) contrasts the institutionalization of some new crimes with the brief fascination with other offenses that don't establish institutional ties.

11. Becker (1995). See also the discussion of inertia in chapter 4.

12. For discussions of different aspects of institutionalization, see Gibbons (1992); Danny Miller and Hartwick (2002); Sterman and Wittenberg (1999); Tyack and Cuban (1995); Zeitz, Mittal, and McAulay (1999).

13. Røvik (1996); Zbaracki (1998).

14. Walt (2000).

15. Benders and van Veen (2001); Zbaracki (1998).

16. Epstein (2002: 175).

17. Røvik (1996: 160).

18. Benders and van Veen (2001).

19. Røvik (1996: 157).

20. Klapp (1991).

21. Peng (1994).

22. Benders and van Veen (2001: 44). On the process in education, see Slavin (1989).

23. John Gill and Whittle (1992: 288).

24. Benders and van Veen (2001). In contrast, the diffusion literature argues that it is late adopters who "are more likely to discontinue innovations than are earlier adopters" (Rogers 1995: 183).

25. While Gladwell (2000) did not originate this term, he brought it into the popular lexicon.

26. E. Abrahamson and Fairchild (1999).

27. Galbraith (1990: 4).

28. Birnbaum (2000); Tyack and Cuban (1995).

29. E. Abrahamson and Fairchild (1999).

30. John Gill and Whittle (1992: 290).

31. Scheirer (1990: 209).

32. Røvik (1996) actually uses all three of these terms.

33. Valentine and Knights (1998).

34. Aguirre (2002); Kieser (1997).

35. Dadds (2001).

36. E. Abrahamson and Fairchild (1999); Lawler and Mohrman (1985); Zbaracki (1998).

37. E. Abrahamson (1991); Kieser (1997). For a related concept, see Wilsnack (1979).

38. E. Abrahamson and Fairchild (1999: 730).

39. Huczynski (1993: 268). Gibson and Tesone (2001: 132) note that experience with one fad "prepares the individual [manager] in a very real way for the next management fad or fashion that is bound to come along."

40. E. Abrahamson and Fairchild (2001: 175).

41. Mapes (1977).

42. Birnbaum (2000); Brindle and Stearns (2001). A leading business process reengineering guru argued that only a tenth of the companies that adopted the program implemented it correctly (Micklethwait and Wooldridge 1996).

43. Benders and van Veen (2001); Hamde (2002); Røvik (1996).

44. Carson et al. (1999); Cuban (1990); Kieser (1997).

45. Tyack and Cuban (1995: 113) call this "strategic silence."

46. Strang and Macy (2001). Greve (1995) offers a rare case study of one fad's demise.

6. Fad Dynamics

1. On California's recent reading policies, see Innes (2002); Krashen (2002); Lemann (1997); Stahl (1999); P. Wolfe and Poynor (2001). For the longer history of the debate, see Chall (1967); Feitelson (1988); M. Mathews (1966).

2. For a thorough analysis of different efforts to diagram the course of various events, see Zerubavel (2003).

3. Cuban (1990). See also Slavin (1989).

4. Hulbert (2003: 364–65).

5. For normative vs. rational control, see E. Abrahamson (1997), Barley and Kunda (1992); for "top-down control" vs. "bottom-up empowerment," see Malone (1997). For other bases for discerning pendulum swings in management, see Brindle and Stearns (2001).

6. The classic analysis of patterns in clothing fashions is Richardson and Kroeber (1940).

7. Robinson (1976).

8. Lieberson (2000).

9. For example, Mahoney and McCue (1999) offer a scheme that classifies management fads into six types.

10. Cuban (1990) notes another problem with the pendulum image: some external force is needed to start a pendulum in motion, but it is not clear what fills this role in the case of institutional fads.

11. Barnett (1995); Fumento (1997); McHenry (1960).

12. Tyack and Cuban (1995) suggest that images of waves or cycles also foster a sense of futility in that both seem inevitable and unstoppable.

13. Hilgartner and Bosk (1988).

14. Lieberson (2000) uses the ratchet as a metaphor, although his account is somewhat different from mine.

15. Tonry (1995).

16. Stinchcomb (1999).

17. Tonry (2004).

18. Galliher and Galliher (1997); Mooney and Lee (1999).

19. Irwin (1980); Rothman (1971, 1980).

20. Gladwell (2000); Suzuki and Best (2003); T. Wolfe (1968).

21. There is a large literature on variations in the rates at which medical diagnoses and procedures occur in different locales. See, for example, Bakwin (1945); Phelps and Mooney (1993); Silverstein (1997).

22. Analysts of style and taste note that these tend to be diverse in contemporary societies. See, for instance, H. Meyer (2000); Postrel (2003).

23. Various analysts have offered versions of the spiral image. See, for example, Czarniawska and Joerges (1996); Khalil (1995); Lofland (1993).

7. Becoming Fad-Proof

1. Ioannidis (2005) found that highly cited medical findings were often contradicted by later research; this was particularly true when the original research did not involve randomized, controlled designs.

2. Critics within many institutions have argued that institutional fads spread because too little weight is placed on evidence. For example, see Slavin (1989) on education, or Robin (1984) on medicine.

3. Young (1967).

4. Analysts vary in the degree to which they view style as a social problem. Some (e.g., Marchand 1985; Dawson 2003) argue that manufacturers introduce design changes in a calculated, manipulative effort to make consumers dissatisfied with their lot and willing to buy things they don't need. For more benign interpretations, see Molotch (2003); Postrel (2003).

References

Abbott, Andrew. 2001. *Chaos of Disciplines.* Chicago: University of Chicago Press.

Abrahamson, Eric. 1991. "Managerial Fads and Fashion." *Academy of Management Review* 16: 586–612.

———. 1996a. "Management Fashion." *Academy of Management Review* 21: 254–85.

———. 1996b. "Technical and Aesthetic Fashion." In *Translating Organizational Change*, edited by Barbara Czarniawska and Guje Sevon, 117–37. Berlin: Walter de Gruyter.

———. 1997. "The Emergence and Prevalence of Employee Management Rhetorics: The Effects of Long Waves, Labor Unions, and Turnover, 1875 to 1992." *Academy of Management Journal* 40: 491–533.

Abrahamson, Eric, and Gregory Fairchild. 1999. "Management Fashion: Lifecycles, Triggers, and Collective Learning Processes." *Administrative Science Quarterly* 44: 708–40.

———. 2001. "Knowledge Industries and Idea Entrepreneurs: New Dimensions of Innovative Products, Services, and Organizations." In *The Entrepreneurship Dynamic*, edited by Claudia Bird Schoonhoven and Elaine Romanelli, 147–77. Stanford, CA: Stanford University Press.

Abrahamson, Eric, and Lori Rosenkopf. 1993. "Institutional and Competitive Bandwagons: Using Mathematical Modeling as a Tool to Explore Innovation Diffusion." *Academy of Management Review* 18: 487–517.

Abrahamson, Warren G., Thomas G. Whitham, and Peter W. Price. 1989. "Fads in Ecology." *BioScience* 39: 321–25.

Adler, Peter. 1981. *Momentum: A Theory of Social Action.* Beverly Hills, CA: Sage.

Aguirre, Benigno E. 2002. "'Sustainable Development' as Collective Surge." *Social Science Quarterly* 83: 101–18.

Aguirre, B. E., E. L. Quarantelli, and Jorge L. Mendoza. 1988. "The Collective Behavior of Fads: The Characteristics, Effects, and Career of Streaking." *American Sociological Review* 53: 569–84.

Aldag, Ramon J. 1997. "Moving Sofas and Exhuming Woodchucks: On Relevance, Impact, and the Following of Fads." *Journal of Management Inquiry* 6 (March): 8–16.

Aronowitz, Robert A. 1998. *Making Sense of Illness: Science, Society, and Disease.* Cambridge: Cambridge University Press.

Bakwin, Harry. 1945. "Pseudodoxia Pediatrica." *New England Journal of Medicine* 232: 691–97.

Barber, Bernard, and Lyle S. Lobel. 1952. "'Fashion' in Women's Clothes and the American Social System." *Social Forces* 31: 124–31.

Barley, Stephen R., and Gideon Kunda. 1992. "Design and Devotion: Surges of Rational and Normative Ideologies of Control in Managerial Discourse." *Administrative Science Quarterly* 37: 363–99.

Barnett, L. Margaret. 1995. "'Every Man His Own Physician': Dietetic Fads, 1890–1914." *Clio Medica* 32: 155–78.

Bauchner, Howard. 1999. "Evidence-Based Medicine: A New Science or an Epidemiologic Fad?" *Pediatrics* 103: 1029–31.

Becker, Howard S. 1995. "The Power of Inertia." *Qualitative Sociology* 18: 301–9.

Benders, Jos, and Kees van Veen. 2001. "What's in a Fashion? Interpretive Viability and Management Fashions." *Organization* 8: 33–53.

Best, Joel. 1999. *Random Violence: How We Talk about New Crimes and New Victims.* Berkeley: University of California Press.

———. 2001. "Social Progress and Social Problems: Toward a Sociology of Gloom." *Sociological Quarterly* 42: 1–12.

Bikhchandani, Sushil, David Hirshleifer, and Ivo Welch. 1992. "A Theory of Fads, Fashion, Custom, and Cultural Change as Informational Cascades." *Journal of Political Economy* 100: 992–1026.

———. 1998. "Learning from the Behavior of Others: Conformity, Fads, and Informational Cascades." *Journal of Economic Perspectives* 12 (Summer): 151–70.

Birnbaum, Robert. 2000. *Management Fads in Higher Education*. San Francisco: Jossey-Bass.

Black, Nick. 1999. "Evidence-Based Surgery: A Passing Fad?" *World Journal of Surgery* 23: 789–93.

Blumberg, Neil. 1999. "The Costs and Consequences of Management Fads and Politically Driven Regulatory Oversight: The Case of Blood Transfusion." *Archives of Pathology and Laboratory Medicine* 123: 580–84.

Blumer, Herbert. 1969. "Fashion: From Class Differentiation to Collective Selection." *Sociological Quarterly* 10: 275–91.

Bogardus, Emory S. 1924. "Social Psychology of Fads." *Journal of Applied Sociology* 8: 239–43.

———. 1950. *Fundamentals of Social Psychology*. 4th ed. New York: Appleton-Century-Crofts.

Bourdieu, Pierre. 1984. *Distinction: A Social Critique of the Judgement of Taste*. Translated by Richard Nice. Cambridge, MA: Harvard University Press.

Boyle, Matthew. 2004. "Atkins World: When Did Carbs Replace Fat as Nutritional Enemy No. 1?" *Fortune* 149 (January 12): 94–96, 98–99, 102, 104.

Brindle, Margaret C., and Peter N. Stearns. 2001. *Facing Up to Management Faddism*. Westport, CT: Quorum.

Bronfenbrenner, Martin. 1966. "Trends, Cycles, and Fads in Economic Writing." *American Economic Review* 56: 538–52.

Brunsma, David L. 2004. *The School Uniform Movement and What It Tells*

Us about American Education: A Symbolic Crusade. Lanham, MD: ScarecrowEducation.

Buchholz, H. E. 1931. *Fads and Fallacies in Present-Day Education.* New York: Macmillan.

Buchholz, Todd G. 1999. *Market Shock: Nine Economic and Social Upheavals That Will Shake Your Financial Future — and What to Do about Them.* New York: HarperCollins.

Burnum, John F. 1987. "Medical Practice à la Mode: How Medical Fashions Determine Medical Care." *New England Journal of Medicine* 317 (November 5): 1220–22.

Campbell, Joseph K., and Cindy Johnson. 1999. "Trend Spotting: Fashions in Medical Education." *British Medical Journal* 318: 1271–75.

Carson, Paula Phillips, Patricia A. Lanier, Kerry David Carson, and Betty J. Birkenmeier. 1999. "A Historical Perspective on Fad Adoption and Abandonment." *Journal of Management History* 5: 320–33.

Carter, Michael. 2003. *Fashion Classics from Carlyle to Barthes.* New York: Berg.

Chall, Jeanne S. 1967. *Learning to Read: The Great Debate.* New York: McGraw-Hill.

Chancellor, Edward. 1999. *Devil Take the Hindmost: A History of Financial Speculation.* New York: Plume.

Clark, Timothy. 2004. "The Fashion of Management Fashion: A Surge Too Far?" *Organization* 11: 297–306.

Clark, Timothy, and David Greatbatch. 2004. "Management Fashion as Image-Spectacle: The Production of Best-Selling Management Books." *Management Communication Quarterly* 17: 396–424.

Clark, Timothy, and Graeme Salaman. 1996. "The Management Guru as Organizational Witchdoctor." *Organization* 3: 85–107.

Cohn, Carole A. 1996. "Mandatory School Uniforms." *School Administrator* 53 (February): 22–25.

Cole, Robert E. 1999. *Managing Quality Fads: How American Business Learned to Play the Quality Game.* New York: Oxford University Press.

Collins, David. 2001. "The Fad Motif in Management Scholarship." *Employee Relations* 23: 26–37.

———. 2003. "The Branding of Management Knowledge: Rethinking Management 'Fads.'" *Journal of Organizational Change Management* 16: 186–204.

Collins, H. M. 2000. "Surviving Closure: Post-Rejection Adaptation and Plurality in Science." *American Sociological Review* 65: 824–45.

Corn, Joseph J., ed. 1986. *Imagining Tomorrow: History, Technology, and the American Future.* Cambridge, MA: MIT Press.

Crane, Diana. 1969. "Fashion in Science: Does It Exist?" *Social Problems* 16: 433–41.

———. 2000. *Fashion and Its Social Agendas.* Chicago: University of Chicago Press.

Cuban, Larry. 1990. "Reforming Again, Again, and Again." *Educational Researcher* 19 (January): 3–13.

Czarniawska, Barbara, and Bernward Joerges. 1996. "Travels of Ideas." In *Translating Organizational Change*, edited by Barbara Czarniawska and Guje Sevon, 13–48. Berlin: Walter de Gruyter.

Dadds, Mark R. 2001. "Fads, Politics, and Research: Keeping Prevention on the Mental Health Agenda." *Prevention and Treatment* 4 (article 6, posted March 30). http://journals.apa.org/prevention/volume4/pre0040006c.html (accessed January 17, 2004).

Davis, Fred. 1992. *Fashion, Culture, and Identity.* Chicago: University of Chicago Press.

Dawson, Michael. 2003. *The Consumer Trap: Big Business Marketing in American Life.* Urbana: University of Illinois Press.

DiMaggio, Paul J., and Walter W. Powell. 1983. "The Iron Cage Revisited: Institutional Isomorphism and Collective Rationality in Organizational Fields." *American Sociological Review* 48: 147–60.

Dundes, Alan, and Carl R. Pagter. 1975. *Urban Folklore from the Paperwork Empire.* Austin, TX: American Folklore Society.

———. 1987. *When You're Up to Your Ass in Alligators: More Urban Folklore from the Paperwork Empire.* Detroit: Wayne State University Press.

———. 1996. *Sometimes the Dragon Wins: Yet More Urban Folklore from the Paperwork Empire.* Syracuse, NY: Syracuse University Press.

―――. 2000. *Why Don't Sheep Shrink When It Rains? A Further Collection of Photocopier Folklore.* Syracuse, NY: Syracuse University Press.

Durkheim, Emile. 1982. *The Rules of Sociological Method.* Edited by Steven Lukes; translated by W. D. Halls. New York: Free Press.

Dychtwald, Ken, and Joe Flower. 1990. *Age Wave: How the Most Important Trend of Our Time Will Change Your Future.* New York: Bantam.

Easterbrook, Gregg. 2003. *The Progress Paradox: How Life Gets Better While People Feel Worse.* New York: Random House.

Emery, James Newell. 1930. "Can the Schools Harness Radio?" *Journal of Education* 112 (October 6): 235–37.

Ennett, Susan T., Nancy S. Tobler, Christopher L. Ringwalt, and Robert L. Flewelling. 1994. "How Effective Is Drug Abuse Resistance Education? A Meta-Analysis of Project DARE Outcome Evaluations." *American Journal of Public Health* 84: 1394–1401.

Epstein, Joseph. 2002. *Snobbery: The American Version.* Boston: Houghton Mifflin.

Feitelson, Dina. 1988. *Facts and Fads in Beginning Reading: A Cross-Language Perspective.* Norwood, NJ: Ablex.

Fell, Honor B. 1960. "Fashion in Cell Biology." *Science* 132: 1625–27.

Field, George A. 1970. "The Status Float Phenomenon: The Upward Diffusion of Innovation." *Business Horizons* 13 (August): 45–52.

Fineman, Stephen. 2001. "Fashioning the Environment." *Organization* 8: 17–31.

Finkelstein, Joanne. 1998. *Fashion: An Introduction.* New York: New York University Press.

Frank, Thomas. 1997. *The Conquest of Cool: Business Culture, Counterculture, and the Rise of Hip Consumerism.* Chicago: University of Chicago Press.

Fumento, Michael. 1997. *The Fat of the Land: The Obesity Epidemic and How Overweight Americans Can Help Themselves.* New York: Viking.

Furnham, Adrian. 2004. *Management and Myths: Challenging Business Fads, Fallacies and Fashions.* Hampshire: Palgrave.

Furusten, Staffan. 1999. *Popular Management Books: How They Are Made and What They Mean for Organizations.* New York: Routledge.

Galbraith, John Kenneth. 1990. *A Short History of Financial Euphoria.* New York: Penguin.

Galliher, James M., and John F. Galliher. 1997. "'Déjà Vu All Over Again': The Recurring Life and Death of Capital Punishment Legislation in Kansas." *Social Problems* 44: 369–85.

Gardner, Martin. 1957. *Fads and Fallacies in the Name of Science.* New York: Dover.

Gibbons, Ann. 1992. "Conservation Biology in the Fast Lane." *Science* 255 (January 3): 20–22.

Gibelman, Margaret. 2004. "Searching for Utopia: The Cycles of Service Provider Preferences." *Administration in Social Work* 28: 137–59.

Gibson, Jane Whitney, and Dana V. Tesone. 2001. "Management Fads: Emergence, Evolution, and Implications for Managers." *Academy of Management Executive* 15, no. 4: 122–33.

Gill, Jag S. 2004. "A Nonfinancial Approach to Financial Improvement of Medical Groups through Advanced Access." *Journal of Healthcare Management* 49: 271–77.

Gill, John, and Sue Whittle. 1992. "Management by Panacea: Accounting for Transience." *Journal of Management Studies* 30: 281–95.

Glaberson, William. 1995. "Article Says 2 Authors Tried to Exploit Times List." *New York Times,* July 28, C2.

Gladwell, Malcolm. 2000. *The Tipping Point: How Little Things Can Make a Big Difference.* Boston: Little, Brown.

Glazer, Sarah. 2000. "Postmodern Nursing." *Public Interest* 140: 3–16.

Goffman, Erving. 1959. *The Presentation of Self in Everyday Life.* Garden City, NY: Doubleday Anchor.

Golf. 2004. "Sphere Factors." July 1, p. 104.

Goode, Erich. 1992. *Collective Behavior.* Fort Worth, TX: Harcourt Brace Jovanovich.

Granovetter, Mark S. 1973. "The Strength of Weak Ties." *American Journal of Sociology* 78: 1360–80.

Greatbatch, David, and Timothy Clark. 2003. "Displaying Group Cohesiveness: Humour and Laughter in the Public Lectures of Management Gurus." *Human Relations* 56: 1515–44.

Greve, Henrich R. 1995. "Jumping Ship: The Diffusion of Strategy Abandonment." *Administrative Science Quarterly* 40: 444–73.

Guillory, John. 2002. "The Sokal Affair and the History of Criticism." *Critical Inquiry* 28: 470–508.

Hacking, Ian. 1995. *Rewriting the Soul: Multiple Personality and the Sciences of Memory.* Princeton, NJ: Princeton University Press.

Hagstrom, Warren O. 1965. *The Scientific Community.* New York: Basic Books.

Hamde, Kiflemariam. 2002. "Teamwork: Fashion or Institution?" *Economic and Industrial Democracy* 23: 389–420.

Hannan, Michael T., and John Freeman. 1984. "Structural Inertia and Organizational Change." *American Sociological Review* 49: 149–64.

Hans, M. G. 2004. "Taking Stock." *Clinical Orthodontics and Research* 7 (August): 143–49.

Hayes, Dade, and Jonathan Bing. 2004. *Open Wide: How Hollywood Box Office Became a National Obsession.* New York: Hyperion.

Healthcare Financial Management. 2004. "Emerging Roles in Revenue Cycle Leadership." *Healthcare Financial Management* 58 (August): 49–54.

Herman, Arthur. 1997. *The Idea of Decline in Western History.* New York: Free Press.

Hilgartner, Stephen, and Charles L. Bosk. 1988. "The Rise and Fall of Social Problems." *American Journal of Sociology* 94: 53–78.

Hirsch, Paul M. 1972. "Processing Fads and Fashions." *American Journal of Sociology* 77: 639–59.

Hirshleifer, David. 1995. "The Blind Leading the Blind: Social Influence, Fads, and Informational Cascades." In *The New Economics of Human Behavior,* edited by Mariano Tommasi and Kathryn Ierulli, 188–215. Cambridge: Cambridge University Press.

Hoffler-Riddick, Pamela Y., and Kathy J. Lassiter. 1996. "No More 'Sag Baggin': School Uniforms Bring the Focus Back to Instruction." *Schools in the Middle* 5 (May): 27–28.

Hoffmann, Frank W., and William G. Bailey. 1990. *Arts and Entertainment Fads.* New York: Haworth.

―――. 1991. *Sports and Recreation Fads*. New York: Haworth.

―――. 1992. *Mind and Society Fads*. New York: Haworth.

―――. 1994. *Fashion and Merchandising Fads*. New York: Haworth.

Hoffmann, Frank W., and Martin Manning. 2002. *Herbal Medicine and Botanical Medical Fads*. New York: Haworth.

Holbrook, M. B. 2002. "Complexity and Management: Fad or Radical Challenge to Systems Thinking?" *Journal of Macromarketing* 22: 198–201.

Howard, Vicki. 2003. "A 'Real Man's Ring': Gender and the Invention of Tradition." *Journal of Social History* 36: 837–56.

Huczynski, Andrezej A. 1993. *Management Gurus: What Makes Them and How to Become One*. New York: Routledge.

Huizenga, John R. 1992. *Cold Fusion: The Scientific Fiasco of the Century*. Rochester, NY : University of Rochester Press.

Hulbert, Ann. 2003. *Raising America: Experts, Parents, and a Century of Advice about Children*. New York: Knopf.

Ingersoll, Richard M. 2003. *Who Controls Teachers' Work? Power and Accountability in America's Schools*. Cambridge, MA: Harvard University Press.

Innes, Richard G. 2002. "There's More Than Mythology to California's Reading Decline." *Phi Delta Kappan* 84: 155–56, 159.

Ioannidis, John P. A. 2005. "Contradicted and Initially Stronger Effects in Highly Cited Clinical Research." *Journal of the American Medical Association* 294: 218–28.

Irwin, John. 1980. *Prisons in Turmoil*. Boston: Little, Brown.

Jackson, Brad. 2001. *Management Gurus and Management Fashions*. New York: Routledge.

Jenness, Valerie, and Ryken Grattet. 2001. *Making Hate a Crime: From Social Movement to Law Enforcement*. New York: Russell Sage Foundation.

Johnson, Richard A. 1985. *American Fads*. New York: Beech Tree Books.

Katz, Elihu, and Paul F. Lazersfeld. 1955. *Personal Influence: The Part Played by People in the Flow of Mass Communications*. New York: Free Press.

Keliher, Evan. 2002. "Forget the Fads—The Old Way Works Best." *Newsweek* 139 (September 30): 18.

Khalil, Elias L. 1995. "Nonlinear Thermodynamics and Social Science Modeling: Fad Cycles, Cultural Development and Identificational Slips." *American Journal of Economics and Sociology* 54: 423–38.

Khurana, Rakesh. 2002. *Searching for a Corporate Savior: The Irrational Quest for Charismatic CEOs.* Princeton, NJ: Princeton University Press.

Kieser, Alfred. 1997. "Rhetoric and Myth in Management Fashion." *Organization* 4: 49–74.

Kindleberger, Charles P. 1978. *Manias, Panics, and Crashes: A History of Financial Crises.* New York: Basic.

Kirchner, Paul. 1995. *Forgotten Fads and Fabulous Flops.* Los Angeles: General Publishing.

Klapp, Orrin E. 1991. *Inflation of Symbols: Loss of Values in American Culture.* New Brunswick, NJ: Transaction.

Knight, Edgar W. 1948. "An Early Educational Fad in the South." *High School Journal* 31: 54–60.

Krashen, Stephen. 2002. "Whole Language and the Great Plummet of 1987–92: An Urban Legend from California." *Phi Delta Kappan* 83: 748–53.

Kuhn, Thomas S. 1962. *The Structure of Scientific Revolutions.* Chicago: University of Chicago Press.

Lamont, Michèle. 1987. "How to Become a Dominant French Philosopher: The Case of Jacques Derrida." *American Journal of Sociology* 93: 584–622.

Langmuir, I. 1953. "Pathological Science." Colloquium at Knolls Research Laboratory, Niskayuna, NY, December 18.

Lasch, Christopher. 1991. *The True and Only Heaven: Progress and Its Critics.* New York: Norton.

Launer, J. 2003. "Narrative-Based Medicine: A Passing Fad or a Giant Leap for General Practice?" *British Journal of General Practice* 53: 91–92.

Lawler, Edward E., III, and Susan A. Mohrman. 1985. "Quality Circles after the Fad." *Harvard Business Review* 63 (January): 65–71.

Lemann, Nicholas. 1997. "The Reading Wars." *Atlantic Monthly* 280 (November): 128–30, 132–34.

Lewis, Bernard. 2002. *What Went Wrong? Western Impact and Middle Eastern Response.* Oxford: Oxford University Press.

Lewis, Philip. 1948. "The Future of Television in Education." *Phi Delta Kappan* 30 (December): 157–60.

Lieberson, Stanley. 2000. *A Matter of Taste: How Names, Fashions, and Culture Change.* New Haven, CT: Yale University Press.

Lipton, Jack P., and Alan M. Hershaft. 1985. "On the Widespread Acceptance of Dubious Medical Findings." *Journal of Health and Social Behavior* 26: 336–51.

Loesch, Paul C. 1995. "A School Uniform Program That Works." *Principal* 74 (March): 28–30.

Lofland, John. 1990. "Collective Behavior: The Elementary Forms." In *Social Psychology: Sociological Perspectives*, edited by Morris Rosenberg and Ralph Turner, 411–46. 2nd ed. New Brunswick, NJ: Transaction.

———. 1993. *Polite Protesters: The American Peace Movement of the 1980s.* Syracuse, NY: Syracuse University Press.

Loseke, Donileen R. 2003. *Thinking about Social Problems.* 2nd ed. Hawthorne, NY: Aldine de Gruyter.

Lutz, William. 1996. *The New Doublespeak: Why No One Knows What Anyone's Saying Anymore.* New York: HarperCollins.

Macfarlane, Alan, and Gerry Martin. 2002. *Glass: A World History.* Chicago: University of Chicago Press.

Mahar, Maggie. 2003. *Bull! A History of the Boom, 1982–1999.* New York: HarperBusiness.

Mahoney, Richard J., and Joseph A. McCue. 1999. "Insights from Business Strategy and Management 'Big Ideas' of the Past Three Decades: Are They Fads or Enablers?" CEO Series no. 19. St. Louis: Washington University Center for the Study of American Business.

Malmi, Teemu. 1999. "Activity-Based Costing Diffusion across Organizations: An Exploratory Empirical Analysis of Finnish Firms." *Accounting, Organizations and Society* 24: 649–72.

Malone, Thomas W. 1997. "Is Empowerment Just a Fad? Control, Decision Making, and IT." *Sloan Management Review* 38 (Winter): 23–35.

Mapes, Roy E. A. 1977. "Physician Drug Innovation and Relinquishment." *Social Science and Medicine* 11: 619–24.

Marchand, Roland. 1985. *Advertising the American Dream: Making Way for Modernity, 1920–1940.* Berkeley: University of California Press.

Martellaro, Helena C. 1980. "What's Keeping Computers Out of the Classroom?" *Creative Computing* 6 (September): 104–5.

Marum, Andrew, and Frank Parise. 1984. *Follies and Foibles: A View of 20th Century Fads.* New York: Facts on File.

Mathews, Jay, and Peter Katel. 1992. "The Cost of Quality." *Newsweek* 120 (September 7): 48–49.

Mathews, Mitford M. 1966. *Teaching to Read, Historically Considered.* Chicago: University of Chicago Press.

McDonald, Clement J. 1996. "Medical Heuristics: The Silent Adjudicators of Clinical Practice." *Annals of Internal Medicine* 124: 56–62.

McHenry, E. W. 1960. *Foods without Fads: A Common Sense Guide to Nutrition.* Philadelphia: Lippincott.

McHugh, Paul R. 1992. "Psychiatric Misadventures." *American Scholar* 20: 497–510.

McPhail, Clark. 2005. "Are Current Campus Riots Just Another Fad?" Paper presented at the annual meeting of the Midwest Sociological Society, Minneapolis.

Mellican, R. Eugene. 1992. "From Fusion Frenzy to Fraud: Reflections on Science and Its Cultural Norms." *Bulletin of the Science and Technology Society* 12: 1–9.

Meyer, Heinz-Dieter. 2000. "Taste Formation in Pluralistic Societies." *International Sociology* 15: 33–56.

Meyer, John W. 2004. "The Nation as Babbitt: How Countries Conform." *Contexts* 3 (Summer): 42–47.

Meyer, John W., and Brian Rowan. 1977. "Institutionalized Organizations: Formal Structure as Myth and Ceremony." *American Journal of Sociology* 83: 340–63.

Meyersohn, Rolf, and Elihu Katz. 1957. "Notes on a Natural History of Fads." *American Journal of Sociology* 62: 594–601.

Micklethwait, John, and Adrian Wooldridge. 1996. *The Witch Doctors: Making Sense of Management Gurus.* New York: Times Books.

Miller, Danny, and Jon Hartwick. 2002. "Spotting Management Fads." *Harvard Business Review* 80 (October): 26–27.

Miller, David L. 2000. *Introduction to Collective Behavior and Collective Action.* 2nd ed. Prospect Heights, IL: Waveland.

Mittelsteadt, Sandra, and Diane Lindsey Reeves. 2003. "Career Academies: Cutting-Edge Reform or Passing Fad?" *Techniques: Connecting Education and Careers* 78 (April): 38–41.

Molotch, Harvey. 2003. *Where Stuff Comes From: How Toasters, Toilets, Cars, Computers, and Many Other Things Come to Be as They Are.* New York: Routledge.

Mooney, Christopher Z., and Mei-Hsien Lee. 1999. "Morality Policy Reinvention: State Death Statutes." *Annals of the American Academy of Political and Social Sciences* 566: 80–92.

Mulhern, Sherrill. 1991. "Satanism and Psychotherapy: A Rumor in Search of an Inquisition." In *The Satanism Scare*, edited by James T. Richardson, Joel Best, and David G. Bromley, 145–72. Hawthorne, NY: Aldine de Gruyter.

Mulligan, Thomas S. 2004. "Another '90s Bad Dream." *Los Angeles Times*, August 26, A1.

Naim, Moises. 2000. "Fads and Fashion in Economic Reforms: Washington Consensus or Washington Confusion?" *Third World Quarterly* 21: 505–28.

Newell, Sue, Jacky Swan, and Maxine Robertson. 1998. "A Cross-National Comparison of the Adoption of Business Process Reengineering: Fashion-Setting Networks?" *Journal of Strategic Information Systems* 7: 299–317.

New York Times. 1915. "As to Wrist Watch, We'll Know Today: Jewelers to Decide Momentous Question of Men's Fashion at Final Session." August 28, p. 9.

Nisbet, Robert. 1980. *The History of the Idea of Progress.* New York: Basic Books.

Panati, Charles. 1991. *Panati's Parade of Fads, Follies, and Manias: The Origins of Most Cherished Obsessions.* New York: HarperCollins.

Park, Robert. 2000. *Voodoo Science: The Road from Foolishness to Fraud.* New York: Oxford University Press.

Peng, Yali. 1994. "Intellectual Fads in Political Science." *PS: Political Science and Politics* (March): 100–108.

Peterson, Peter G. 2000. *Gray Dawn: How the Coming Age Wave Will Transform America — and the World.* New York: Three Rivers.

Phelps, Charles E., and Cathleen Mooney. 1993. "Variations in Medical Practice Use: Causes and Consequences." In *Competitive Approaches to Health Care Reform,* edited by Richard J. Arnould, Robert F. Rich, and William D. White, 139–78. Washington, DC: Urban Institute Press.

Placier, Margaret. 1996. "The Cycle of Student Labels in Education: The Cases of *Culturally Deprived/Disadvantaged* and *At Risk.*" *Educational Administration Quarterly* 32: 236–70.

Placier, Margaret, Michael Walker, and Bill Foster. 2002. "Writing the 'Show-Me' Standards: Teacher Professionalism and Political Control in U.S. Curriculum Policy." *Curriculum Inquiry* 32: 281–310.

Postrel, Virginia. 2003. *The Substance of Style: How the Rise of Aesthetic Value Is Remaking Commerce, Culture, and Consciousness.* New York: HarperCollins.

Powell, Charles A. 1968. "Simulation: The Anatomy of a Fad." *Acta Politica* 4: 299–330.

Ravitch, Diane. 2000. *Left Back: A Century of Failed School Reforms.* New York: Simon and Schuster.

Redway, Jacques W. 1896. "The Psychology of Educational Fads." *Educational Review* 11: 179–81.

Richardson, Jane, and A. L. Kroeber. 1940. "Three Centuries of

Women's Dress Fashions: A Quantitative Analysis." *Anthropological Records* 5: 111–53.

Richman, Judith A., and Leonard A. Jason. 2001. "Gender Biases Underlying the Social Construction of Illness States: The Case of Chronic Fatigue Syndrome." *Current Sociology* 49 (May): 15–29.

Robin, Eugene D. 1984. *Matters of Life and Death: Risks vs. Benefits of Medical Care.* New York: W. H. Freeman.

———. 1985. "The Cult of the Swan-Ganz Catheter: Overuse and Abuse of Pulmonary Flow Catheters." *Annals of Internal Medicine* 103: 445–49.

Robinson, Dwight E. 1976. "Fashions in Shaving and Trimming of the Beard: The Men of the *Illustrated London News*, 1842–1972." *American Journal of Sociology* 81: 1133–41.

Rogers, Everett M. 1995. *Diffusion of Innovations.* 4th ed. New York: Free Press.

Rothman, David J. 1971. *The Discovery of the Asylum: Social Order and Disorder in the New Republic.* Boston: Little, Brown.

———. 1980. *Conscience and Convenience: The Asylum and Its Alternatives in Progressive America.* Boston: Little, Brown.

Rourke, James R. 2001. "Online Learning: Fad or Fate?" *Principal Leadership* 1 (May): 8, 10–14.

Røvik, Kjell Arne. 1996. "Deinstitutionalization and the Logic of Fashion." In *Translating Organizational Change,* edited by Barbara Czarniawska and Guje Sevon, 139–71. Berlin: Walter de Gruyter.

Rozhon, Tracie. 2002. "Is It Over? Real Estate Boom May Be Easing, Signs Show." *New York Times,* November 10, sec. 1, 43.

Sandage, Scott A. 2005. *Born Losers: A History of Failure in America.* Cambridge, MA: Harvard University Press.

Sapir, Edward. 1931. "Fashion." In *Encyclopaedia of the Social Sciences,* 6:139–44. New York: Macmillan.

Sarason, Seymour B. 1990. *The Predictable Failure of Educational Reform: Can We Change Course Before It's Too Late?* San Francisco: Jossey-Bass.

———. 1996. *Revisiting "The Culture of the School and the Problem of Change."* New York: Teachers College Press.

Scheirer, Mary Ann. 1990. "The Life Cycle of an Innovation: Adoption versus Discontinuation of the Fluoride Mouth Rinse Program in Schools." *Journal of Health and Social Behavior* 31: 203–15.

Shao, Maria. 1995. "Beyond Reengineering." *Boston Globe*, November 12, A121.

Sharkey, Joe. 2003. "Business Travel: On the Road." *New York Times*, July 8, C7.

Shiller, Robert J. 2000. *Irrational Exuberance*. Princeton, NJ: Princeton University Press.

Showalter, Elaine. 1997. *Hystories: Hysterical Epidemics and Modern Media*. New York: Columbia University Press.

Silverman, Rachel. 2000. "The Blood Group 'Fad' in Post-War Racial Anthropology." *Kroeber Anthropological Society Papers* 84: 11–27.

Silverstein, Arthur M. 1997. "Changing Trends in the Etiologic Diagnosis of Uveitis." *Documenta Ophthalmologica* 94: 25–37.

Simmel, Georg. [1904] 1957. "Fashion." *American Journal of Sociology* 62: 541–58.

Simon, Bart. 2002. *Undead Science : Science Studies and the Afterlife of Cold Fusion*. New Brunswick, NJ: Rutgers University Press.

Simon, Ralph, and Gilles Babinet. 2004. "Mobile Music." *Billboard*, June 5, p. 9.

Sims, Joel K. 2001. "Green Schools: A Design Fad or a Trend Worth Embracing?" *School Planning and Management* 40 (March): 25–26, 28–30.

Slavin, Robert E. 1989. "PET and the Pendulum: Faddism in Education and How to Stop It." *Phi Delta Kappan* 70: 752–58.

Smith, Martin J., and Patrick J. Kiger. 2004. *Poplorica: A Popular History of the Fads, Mavericks, Inventions, and Lore That Shaped Modern America*. New York: HarperCollins.

Sommer, Robert. 1974. *Tight Spaces: Hard Architecture and How to Humanize It*. Englewood Cliffs, NJ: Prentice-Hall.

Soule, Sarah A. 1999. "The Diffusion of an Unsuccessful Innovation." *Annals of the American Academy of Political and Social Sciences* 566: 120–31.

Spell, Chester S. 1999. "Where Do Management Fashions Come From, and How Long Do They Stay?" *Journal of Management History* 5: 334–48.

———. 2001. "Management Fashions: Where Do They Come From, and Are They Old Wine in New Bottles?" *Journal of Management Inquiry* 10: 358–73.

Stahl, Steven A. 1999. "Why Innovations Come and Go (and Mostly Go): The Case of Whole Language." *Educational Researcher* 28 (November): 13–22.

Steinberg, Neil. 2004. *Hatless Jack: The President, the Fedora, and the History of an American Style.* New York: Plume.

Stensaker, Bjorn. 1998. "Culture and Fashion in Reform Implementation: Perceptions and Adaptation of Management Reforms in Higher Education." *Journal of Higher Education Policy and Management* 20: 129–38.

Sterman, John D., and Jason Wittenberg. 1999. "Path Dependence, Competition, and Succession in the Dynamics of Scientific Revolution." *Organization Science* 10: 322–41.

Stern, Sydney Ladensohn, and Ted Schoenhaus. 1990. *Toyland: The High-Stakes Game of the Toy Industry.* Chicago: Contemporary Books.

Stewart, Thomas A. 1993. "Reengineering: The Hot New Managing Tool." *Fortune* 128 (August 23): 40–43, 46, 48.

Stinchcomb, Jeanne B. 1999. "Recovering from the Shocking Reality of Shock Incarceration—What Correctional Administrators Can Use from Boot Camp Failures." *Correction Management Quarterly* 3, no. 4: 43–52.

Strang, David, and Michael W. Macy. 2001. "In Search of Excellence: Fads, Success Stories, and Adaptive Emulation." *American Journal of Sociology* 107: 147–82.

Strang, David, and John W. Meyer. 1993. "Institutional Conditions for Diffusion." *Theory and Society* 22: 487–511.

Suzuki, Tadashi, and Joel Best. 2003. "The Emergence of Trendsetters for Fashions and Fads: Kogaru in 1990s Japan." *Sociological Quarterly* 44: 61–79.

Taub, Eric. A. 2004. "How Do I Love Thee, TiVo?" *New York Times*, March 18, G1.

Toffler, Alvin. 1970. *Future Shock*. New York: Random House.

Tonry, Michael. 1995. *Malign Neglect: Race, Crime, and Punishment in America*. New York: Oxford University Press.

———. 2004. *Thinking about Crime: Sense and Sensibility in American Penal Culture*. New York: Oxford University Press.

Tyack, David, and Larry Cuban. 1995. *Tinkering toward Utopia: A Century of Public School Reform*. Cambridge, MA: Harvard University Press.

Valentine, Rob, and David Knights. 1998. "TQM and BPR: Can You Spot the Difference?" *Personnel Review* 27: 78–85.

Wahl, Grant. 2004. "The Gods Must Be Crazy." *Sports Illustrated*, July 12, p. 68.

Walt, Stephen M. 2000. "Fads, Fevers, and Firestorms." *Foreign Policy* 121 (November): 34–42.

Warner, Kee, and Harvey Molotch. 1993. "Information in the Marketplace: Media Explanations of the '87 Crash." *Social Problems* 40: 167–88.

Weber, Max. 1946. "Class, Status, Party." In *From Max Weber: Essays in Sociology*, 180–95. Translated and edited by H. H. Gerth and C. Wright Mills. New York: Oxford University Press.

Weick, Karl B. 1976. "Educational Organizations as Loosely Coupled Systems." *Administrative Science Quarterly* 21: 1–19.

Wejnert, Barbara. 2002. "Integrating Models of Diffusion of Innovations: A Conceptual Framework." *Annual Review of Sociology* 28: 297–326.

Welch, H. Gilbert, and Juliana Mogielnicki. 2002. "Presumed Benefit: Lessons from the American Experience with Marrow Transplantation for Breast Cancer." *British Medical Journal* 324: 1088–92.

Westphal, James D., Ranjay Gulati, and Stephen M. Shortell. 1997. "Customization or Conformity? An Institutional and Network Perspective on the Content and Consequences of TQM Adoption." *Administrative Science Quarterly* 42: 366–94.

Wilsnack, Richard W. 1979. "Counterfads: Episodes of Collective Disbelief." Paper presented at the annual meeting of the American Sociological Association, Boston.

Wolfe, Paula, and Leslie Poynor. 2001. "Politics and the Pendulum: An Alternative Understanding of the Case of Whole Language as Educational Innovation." *Educational Researcher* 30: 15–20.

Wolfe, Tom. 1968. *The Pump House Gang.* New York: Farrar, Straus and Giroux.

———. 1970. *Radical Chic and Mau-Mauing the Flak Catchers.* New York: Farrar, Straus and Giroux.

Wysong, Earl, Richard Aniskiewicz, and David Wright. 1994. "Truth and DARE: Tracking Drug Education to Graduation and as Symbolic Politics." *Social Problems* 41: 448–72.

Yonan, Joe. 2005. "Ding-Dong, the Craze Is Dead." *Boston Globe*, March 30, E1.

Young, James Harvey. 1967. *The Medical Messiahs: A Social History of Health Quackery in Twentieth-Century America.* Princeton, NJ: Princeton University Press.

Zbaracki, Mark J. 1998. "The Rhetoric and Reality of Total Quality Management." *Administrative Science Quarterly* 43: 602–36.

Zeitz, Gerald, Vikas Mittal, and Brian McAulay. 1999. "Distinguishing Adoption and Entrenchment of Management Practices: A Framework for Analysis." *Organization Studies* 20: 741–76.

Zerubavel, Evitar. 2003. *Time Maps: Collective Memory and the Social Shape of the Past.* Chicago: University of Chicago Press.

Zorn, Dirk M. 2004. "Here a Chief, There a Chief: The Rise of the CFO in the American Firm." *American Sociological Review* 69: 345–64.

Index

Compositor:	BookMatters, Berkeley
Illustrator:	Bill Nelson
Text:	10/15 Janson
Display:	Folio
Printer and binder:	Thomson-Shore, Inc.